Foreign Investments and the Management of Political Risk

Other Titles in This Series

Westview Special Studies in International Economics and Business

Foreign Investments
and the Management of Political Risk
Dan Haendel

This volume focuses on the efforts that multinational enterprises (MNEs) can and must make to evaluate and deal with the political risks they confront in host countries. After discussing various aspects of the relationships between MNEs and host countries, the author considers the definitional and conceptual issues of political risk. He examines the techniques and information sources currently used by MNEs for political forecasting and analysis and seeks to bridge the gap between political analysis and the realities of business operations through a cash flow approach.

Haendel argues that systematic analysis of political risk must be undertaken by MNEs. He suggests methods for monitoring political risk, as well as corporate strategies for dealing with the phenomenon, and also discusses such controversial issues as terrorism and corporate bribery.

Dan Haendel is currently a fellow at the Georgetown University Center for Strategic and International Studies. His previous publications include *The Process of Priority Formulation: U.S. Foreign Policy in the Indo-Pakistani War of 1971.*

Foreign Investments and the Management of Political Risk

Dan Haendel

Foreword by Amos A. Jordan

Westview Press / Boulder, Colorado

Westview Special Studies in
International Economics and Business

Copyright © 1979 by Westview Press, Inc.

Published in 1979 in the United States of America by
Westview Press, Inc.
5500 Central Avenue
Boulder, Colorado 80301
Frederick A. Praeger, Publisher

Library of Congress Cataloging in Publication Data
Haendel, Dan, 1950-
  Foreign investments and the management of political risk.
  (Westview special studies in international economics and business)
  Includes bibliographical references and index.
  1. Investments, Foreign. 2. International business enterprises. I. Title. II. Title:
Political risk. III. Series.
HG4538.H23   658.1'8   78-13274
ISBN 0-89158-253-3

Printed and bound in the United States of America

To Ellen

Contents

Figures

Tables

Foreword

Fundamental changes have been occurring recently in the international environment within which business decisions must be made. Corporate business leaders involved in overseas investments and operations need, therefore, to keep themselves informed about the changing nature of both international affairs and host societies and governments.

In this work, Dan Haendel, first of all, has carefully and thoughtfully examined the political risk dimensions of international business operations. In addition to dealing with various aspects of risk, he discusses the relationships among MNEs, host governments, and the U.S. government and reviews a number of approaches that several MNEs currently use and that other MNEs can adapt to their particular needs in order to assess their exposure to political factors. Furthermore, he analyzes methods through which foreign investors can conduct their enterprises so as to manage political risk. Each of these aspects of the conduct of international business has important implications for the international business manager who must make decisions affecting the viability and profitability of the enterprise.

Dan Haendel brings a strong and diverse academic, business, and legal background to the subject of business-government relations. He has received a Ph.D., J.D., and M.B.A. from the University of Pennsylvania Graduate School, Law School, and the Wharton School. He has also worked on the staff of Citicorp, in private legal practice, in government, and in policy research institutions.

Since this volume presents and synthesizes much of the available research on political risk for business, it is of great importance to international business executives and government leaders. I recommend it to business and government leaders as well as to students of international relations and business.

Amos A. Jordan
Executive Director, Center for Strategic
and International Studies
Georgetown University

Preface

In 1975 Gerald West, Robert Meadow, and I wrote a monograph entitled *Overseas Investment and Political Risk.* Since that time I have enjoyed the opportunity of participating in the ongoing Wharton School–sponsored seminar entitled "Risk Management of Foreign Investments and Operations." During these seminars I have benefited from the insights of business executives too numerous to mention individually.

Because of the spate of political risk writings and research that have appeared since 1975, the purpose of this book is to update and expand the monograph that launched our efforts. Many of the factors that motivated the research for the monograph have also prompted me to write this book. For example, congressional hearings were held on the Overseas Private Insurance Corporation (OPIC) during 1973 and 1974 and again in 1977 and 1978. In addition, such issues as the role and power of the multinational enterprise (MNE), U.S. government insurance and support of foreign investments, and relations among the MNE, the host country, and the home country remain unresolved.

During the late 1960s several members of the academic community conducted research and published articles on the subject of political risk. The expropriatory actions in Castro's Cuba served to highlight the more dramatic dimension of political risk.[1] However, the 1971 expropriations in Chile and the energy crisis have demonstrated the vulnerabilities of U.S. foreign investments and trade.

The emphasis of this book is on the political risk dimension of foreign investments. However, this issue has many aspects that require consideration. Consequently, we will give particular attention to the various problems the MNE encounters in its foreign investments and operations.

I would like to take this opportunity to thank Ambassador William R. Kintner of the Foreign Policy Research Institute, which sponsored the research on the original monograph. Franklin R. Root of the Wharton School and Gerald West have been helpful colleagues during the presentation of our seminars. My new and current affiliation with the Georgetown University Center for Strategic and International Studies has been of substantial benefit to my research. My special thanks go to Robert A. Kilmarx and Amos A. Jordan. I owe a debt of gratitude to Gregory Wolfe, Millidge Walker, and Jack Piotrow for giving me the opportunity to teach courses on MNEs at the American University School of International Service. Of course, all faults and errors in this work are my responsibility.

I would like to express my special appreciation to my brother Doron for preparing the figures and charts of this book. My parents and sister Varda have been extremely supportive by their encouragement.

Ellen deserves my gratitude for her patience. That she is a business executive in her own right makes my effort easier.

Dan Haendel

Foreign Investments and the
Management of Political Risk

Introduction

Accelerating changes in global politics and economics have highlighted the importance of the U.S. government's policies in the international business arena. Political turbulence has been, and will probably continue to be, reflected in the following two areas: (1) more domestic political violence and antiforeign investment attitudes in the less developed countries (LDCs),[1] and (2) great flux in the structure of international trade and investment as the Third World seeks to change the basis on which international trade and investment is conducted.

The energy crisis, for example, has exposed the U.S. economy's dependence on imported raw materials and, more importantly, has demonstrated the changing pattern of U.S. economic relations with the Third World. Only about one-third of the world's trade is between the industrialized and Third World countries, but this trade is much more important than that figure indicates. The United States is sharply dependent on foreign supplies of raw materials. More than 90 percent of the bauxite, chrome, cobalt, manganese, platinum group metals, and tin used in the United States is imported from foreign sources. In addition, more than 75 percent of the antimony, fluorspar, gold, and nickel; more than 50 percent of the silver, zinc, and cadmium; more than 25 percent of the iron ore, petroleum, and lead ore; and more than 20 percent of the copper and mercury consumed in the United States come from overseas. Many other metals and various foodstuffs of great importance to the United States must also be imported. The relatively high percentage of critical raw materials that is supplied to the United States by South Africa demonstrates the sensitivity of assuring an adequate supply of such resources. The overall U.S. dependence on foreign sources of critical raw materials will doubtlessly continue to increase in the future.

The United States is becoming primarily an exporter of advanced-technology products and foodstuffs and an importer of raw materials and semimanufactured goods. The U.S.-based multinational enterprise (MNE) has become the primary conduit for the export of capital, advanced technology, and entrepreneurial skills to the LDCs and for the import of foodstuffs such as coffee, tea, and sugar, raw materials, and semimanufactured goods from the LDCs.

For a variety of reasons, including a lower level of political risk, U.S.-based MNEs initially looked toward other developed countries for raw materials. In 1970, for example, the industrialized countries exported more primary products to other industrialized countries than did the LDCs. But, driven by the growing scarcity in industrialized countries of certain raw materials and by the economics of extracting them, MNEs involved in extractive industries have been increasingly drawn to the LDCs. Some MNEs, however, prefer to operate in industrialized countries like Canada and Australia, even though they could extract the same minerals far less expensively in various LDCs. The major reason they do so is the political uncertainty they face in the LDCs. Nevertheless, U.S.-based MNEs have been attracted to the LDCs not only by raw materials and the lure of foreign markets but also by investment opportunities and the opportunity of establishing production affiliates.

During the last three decades, many Third World countries have experienced accelerating forces of nationalism mixed with various forms of socialism. These developments have raised the political risk faced by investors and have generated complex dilemmas for both corporations and the U.S. government. With the gradual decline in U.S. foreign assistance over the last decade, the U.S. government has sought, for both humanitarian and developmental reasons, to encourage American private investment in the LDCs. However, many corporations are unwilling to make such investments without some form of "protection" against political risk. Having learned the bitter lesson that direct government intervention on behalf of U.S. corporations usually has the effect, if anything, of encouraging the forces of economic nationalism and anti-American sentiment in the LDC, the U.S. government has adopted the position that "protection" can best be provided through government insurance against such political risks as war, expropriation, and the inconvertibility of assets. Given the underlying conflict among U.S. goals—to aid the development of the LDCs, to encourage U.S. private investment in LDCs, to assure the supply of crucial raw materials, and to lessen the confrontation between LDCs and MNEs—the proper role, if any, for the government and its policies for insuring private investment in the LDCs have become matters of controversy.

The 1971 expropriations of several major U.S. corporations operating in Chile and their claims for approximately $250 million in compensation under provisions of insurance contracts with the Overseas Private Investment Corporation (OPIC) drew widespread public attention to the fact that the United States has for some time provided insurance to U.S. investors against "political risks." The 1973-1974 legislative review of OPIC by both the House and the Senate drew further attention to OPIC's activities and prompted considerable debate over its aims and policies.[2] The main thrust of the 1973 and 1974 congressional hearings was the mandate to OPIC that it implement a "privatization" policy, that is, transfer its insurance portfolio to the private political risk insurance market. But the 1977 congressional review indicated that the "privatization" effort has met with failure.[3] Accordingly, congressional emphasis has been placed on the developmental aspect of OPIC's functions and placing limitations on OPIC's activities.

The proponents and opponents of OPIC have "recruited" several members of the academic community to testify before Congress concerning their research on political risk and OPIC activities. Many in the business community are concerned with the limitations being placed on OPIC's programs because of the increasing costs and risks that will have to be borne by American corporations; they are uneasy with prospects that OPIC's programs will be severely curtailed or that OPIC itself will be abolished in the near future. Many see the restrictions as a manifestation of a larger issue, namely, the extent to which the

U.S. government is willing and able to support U.S.-based corporations that do business in the international arena. This broader issue is particularly significant in light of the various assistance programs sponsored by the Japanese and German governments, for example, for corporations based in those countries. The controversy regarding OPIC, however, has focused on defining the options before, and determining the proper role of, the U.S. government in assisting and fostering private investment in the LDCs, as well as on "protecting" the interests of U.S. investors there.

The debate has recently centered on such questions as what kind of insurance and other programs, if any, the U.S. government can and should provide, which corporations should be eligible for such programs, and in which of the LDCs the programs should operate. Generally, the trend of placing a greater share of the political risk burden on the corporate foreign investor has been rather easy to discern. The various congressional hearings on OPIC and the laws that have emerged from them clearly reflect the limitations being placed on OPIC activities. The blunt message of the Overseas Private Investment Law of 1974 is that in the future the American foreign investor will generally have to shoulder a greater proportion of the political risk he faces. Despite the termination of the "privatization" mandate, the 1978 legislation merely serves to buttress that blunt message by placing various restrictions on OPIC's activities. Political risk may continue to be transferable, but in the future the corporate foreign investor may have only the option of transferring his political risk to the private insurance industry, which, unfortunately, now has a rather low capacity to insure. In confronting a political risk, the MNEs may choose to act as self-insurers or, if possible, to transfer their risk in whole or part to the U.S. government, to the private insurance market, or to some combination of the two. In any event, corporate decision makers will generally have more and more need for an accurate assessment of the political risks they face.

Many U.S.-based MNEs have become acutely aware that political events and developments have influenced their operations. Some have begun to assess systematically the profitability as well as cash availability that result from political events, and they are learning that their political risk analysis must be custom-tailored to their own particular needs and operations. The framework of analysis an MNE should use depends on such factors as its ratio of foreign to domestic investments, the political sensitivity of the industry to which it belongs, and its overall foreign diversification. Therefore, the categories it should consider in its analytical framework will differ according to its particular operations.

War, expropriation, and the inconvertibility of assets—the insurable risks recognized by OPIC—are only three of the nonfinancial risks that confront an investor in overseas investments and operations. Because of the higher uncertainty that corporate executives attach to their investments in LDCs, nonfinancial risks may take on a greater significance for investments undertaken in the LDCs. Moreover, many of these risks are uniquely dependent on the nature and size of an investment. This highlights one of the difficulties faced by political risk analysts—namely, that the implications of the term *political risk* vary with the interests and need of the definer. A private insurance firm, a minerals extractive company, a multinational bank, and a manufacturing enterprise are likely to define political risk quite differently. OPIC itself has its own definition of political risk. The following is the working definition of political risk used in the 1975 monograph: "The political risk faced by foreign investors is defined as the risk or *probability* of occurrence of some political event(s) that will change the prospects for the profitability of a given investment."[4]

To illustrate how a foreign investor may change this definition, consider this version espoused by one major MNE in the extractive sector that is concerned about additional political risk factors like repatriation of profits: "Political risk is the risk or probability of occurence of some political event that will affect the cash available to the shareholders from the corporation's investment in a project."

Although the need for accurate political risk assessment is rising, there is general agreement among both theorists and decision makers in the government, investment, financial, and insurance communities that our knowledge and tools are inadequate to the task. One of the major weaknesses of political risk analysis is that the efforts made in political science and business research have not been integrated. Furthermore, much of the academic research conducted on political risk is not applicable to particular investment and operation decisions being undertaken by foreign corporate investors. This book is an attempt to improve our general understanding of political risk through a review of the subject and of the "services" provided by numerous peddlers of political risk analysis. By examining a variety of ideas on political risk within the covers of a single book, we hope to provide some insights for individual corporate needs in this area. In addition, the book may properly be viewed as a modest attempt to contribute to the formulation of better corporate and public policy.

Chapter 1 deals rather extensively with the position of the multinational enterprise in the international business arena, specifically with the relations between the MNEs and LDCs. Chapter 2 focuses on the role of the U.S. government in the MNE-LDC relationship, the history and functions of the U.S. Investment Insurance Program, and the role of the private insurance industry. In an effort to clarify the term *political risk*, Chapter 3 examines some of the conceptual confusion that surrounds the subject and reviews several frameworks and models proposed for the analysis of political risk. Chapter 4 describes several political risk "services" provided by some consultants on this subject and evaluates some of the efforts undertaken in this field in terms of implementation to specific data. Chapter 5, "Monitoring and Integrating Political Risk," and Chapter 6, "The Management of Political Risk," suggest steps MNEs may take in order to limit their exposure to political risk. A possible approach for monitoring political risk and integrating it with political risk analysis is also presented in this section.

1
Cooperation and Conflict: The MNEs, LDCs, and the United States

During the 1950s and 1960s U.S.-based multinational enterprises (MNEs) experienced a phenomenal rate of growth. This expansion resulted largely from investments in industrialized countries rather than from investments in the less developed countries (LDCs). Since 1971, however, the rate of expansion has declined markedly.[1]

The global recession of the mid-1970s has significantly lowered the expectations of corporate earnings and returns on both domestic and foreign investments. The LDCs have been viewed as increasingly risky, perhaps because of the decline of the market price for many of their key raw materials as well as the increased political turbulence in the world generally. For multinational enterprises seeking to generate profits in the current era of low economic growth, complete information about their foreign investment environment is likely to have a substantial impact on their earnings and corporate strength.

U.S. corporations usually view foreign investments as riskier than investments in the United States, in large part because of the uncertainty of the political environment in the host country. In fact, Henry Kissinger has noted the importance of this factor by suggesting that the development of some ground rules within which private investment can operate is the key to expanding private investment in the LDCs.[2]

Since World War II, business conditions have fluctuated markedly in many countries of the world, particularly in the LDCs. Much of this fluctuation can be attributed to underlying political factors. In many LDCs the drive to stimulate the growth of the gross national product (GNP) has often led to policies unfavorable to international investment. These measures have included (1) the expropriation of public utilities; (2) government investment in, and subsidies for, "bottleneck" industries; (3) agricultural reform; (4) restrictions on imports, exports, and capital flows; (5) requirements on reinvestment of profits and on the ratio of foreign to domestic equity; (6) compulsory subcontracting, as well as a number of steps that many of these states consider essential.

The business environment in many LDCs has also been influenced by a number of other politically inspired factors. New wage and labor laws—frequently enforced in particular against foreign-owned enterprises—have driven up costs, often while real dollar profits have been held constant either by government restrictions or by continuing inflationary spirals and devaluations. Basic shifts in political philosophy—from the loose capitalism of the colonial era to a welfare state philosophy—have taken their toll on investors—for example, the confiscations in Chile, Peru, and Cuba. In other countries, such as Argentina, Uruguay, and Libya, external conflicts and domestic turbulence have victimized not only holdings but also the very lives of MNE personnel.

The list of politically induced investment and business losses is extensive. However, there is an almost equally long list of large and windfall profits resulting from political decisions—such as tax holidays, attractive exemptions from other restrictions, and subsidies from governments interested in attracting industry.

The mounting record of investment losses and failures notwithstanding, few companies conduct much political risk analysis. Among those that do, evaluations tend to be based on such simplistic distinctions as to whether a country is considered "safe" and its leaders "friendly" to the United States. Clearly, however, the political issues that affect foreign investors frequently have little to do with the country's system of government or its liking for the U.S. government.

The initial reaction of a good businessman when faced with an unacceptable risk is to avoid it completely. If he does decide to confront it, he will probably seek either to reduce that risk or to transfer the burden to a third party. For many years U.S.

corporations were relieved of some political risk by "gunboat diplomacy" and other forms of government intervention. Some corporations, especially in Latin America, also used direct methods to reduce political risk. When methods of direct intervention became more and more counterproductive, American businessmen sought other government sanctions to deter threats to their investments abroad. For example, the Hickenlooper and Gonzalez amendments, respectively, mandate an aid cutoff or a negative vote by the United States on loan applications in international financial institutions against a country that expropriates a U.S. firm without just compensation.

In the postwar era, a coincidence of the broad economic interests of the American business community and the political interests of the U.S. government, such as the rebuilding of the war-shattered countries of Western Europe and Japan, led in 1948 to a government insurance program. The types of risks covered by the program were gradually expanded so that the Agency for International Development (AID) was eventually offering insurance to private U.S. investors against the risks of inconvertibility of assets, expropriation, and war, revolution, or insurrection.

During the 1950s and 1960s this insurance program was extended to cover investments in the LDCs as well. In the Foreign Assistance Act of 1969, Congress authorized the creation of OPIC, which assumed operation of AID's private investment incentive programs, including the insurance program. OPIC's overall purpose, as defined in that act, was to "mobilize and facilitate the participation of U.S. private capital and skills in the economic and social progress of less developed friendly countries and areas, thereby complementing the development assistance objectives of the United States." OPIC has sought to make investment in LDCs more attractive by enabling U.S. investors to view investment there on a more competitive basis with alternative opportunities in more developed areas. Thus, OPIC seeks to serve directly the government's dual policy goals. It provides a form of assistance to the developing countries by assisting in the flow of U.S. investment, especially capital investment; at the same time, it seeks to ensure that the United States maintains both its market share in these developing economies and an adequate supply of raw materials.

The availability of relatively inexpensive insurance has enabled some MNEs to concentrate on the purely economic risks they face in foreign investment and to pay less attention to the problem of political risk. As a result, the tools they use to gauge the economic costs and benefits of proposed foreign investments have become relatively well developed and sophisticated. By the same token, the tools they use to analyze the political "costs and benefits" of proposed investments can only be described as primitive.

Partly because of the lack of demand, the academic community has had little motivation to develop analytical tools useful in attacking the problem of political risk to foreign investments. Political scientists have virtually ignored the problem. What little scholarly writing there has been on the subject has generally come from professors of business who have recognized the growing importance of the problem. This does not mean that the would-be investor, worried about political threats to his investment, cannot find help. There is no shortage of people willing to sell their services. Former intelligence and Foreign Service officers, consulting firms, and "confidential" newsletters, for example, are abundantly available. If the would-be investor is willing to devote the time, he can get a mass of data and opinion from various government bodies, such as the Departments of the Treasury, Commerce, and State. His problem, then, is how to separate the relevant from the irrelevant and to come up with a synthesis requisite to *his particular* needs. In other words, data are useless— and quite often debilitatingly confusing—unless there is a framework for applying them. And that framework must be custom-tailored to the firm's exposure. Even though there has been an increased effort to tackle the political risk problem, some of these attempts leave many corporate executives unsatisfied. We will present various efforts in Chapter 4, with particular emphasis on works that seek to bridge the gap between political analysis and the needs and concerns of foreign investors.

The problem for the investor is compounded by the fact that everyone has his own interpretation of "political risk." Moreover, OPIC's focus on inconvertibility, expropriation, and war risks has tended to obscure the many "lesser" political risks that may seriously threaten an investment—the more or less subtle changes in a host country's political conditions that can significantly affect the investment climate.

In short, the study of political risk has been blocked by complacency, confusion, and an inordinate preoccupation with the "cataclysmic" risks—all to the detriment of a concerted approach to the broader problem. But the Overseas Private Investment Act of 1974 indicated a likely change in attitudes. Because they would shoulder a greater portion of the risk burden, corporate investors would have to pay more attention to a rigorous assessment of political risk. Since OPIC is legally required to transfer some of its insurance functions to the private insurance industry, the latter now has to improve its ability to analyze, define, measure, and forecast political risk. Even though the "privatization" mandate has been terminated, the congressional restrictions on OPIC and the limited capacity of the private insurance industry in essence force the MNEs to act as self-insurers. Consequently, the MNEs must themselves undertake explicit and systematic analysis and management of their political risk.

Clashing Interests of the MNEs and LDCs

In this chapter, we explore the economic and political relationships between MNEs and LDCs that give rise to the need for a more systematic method to evaluate, measure, and forecast political events that affect investment considerations. One actual corporate experience is useful in introducing the discussion of MNE-LDC relations.

The experience of Dow Chemical Company in Chile during the Allende period is a dramatic illustration of how one corporation assessed and calculated political risk, dealt with uncertainty, responded to political challenges, and modified its decision-making processes in view of this experience.[3] At the invitation of the Christian Democratic government, Dow contracted in 1966 to build a plastics complex, Petrodow, in a joint venture with the Chilean government. In 1970, as the plastics plant neared completion, Salvador Allende was elected president of Chile. The president of Dow Latin America, David Schornstein, reacted to the news by purchasing a copy of Karl Marx's *Communist*

Manifesto to "refresh his memory about their attitudes." As a decision-maker, he had to choose whether to continue pouring money into Chile or to cut Dow's losses and liquidate the enterprise. The argument that Dow would not be able to operate effectively in Chile if Allende came to power and that Dow should therefore cut its operation was rejected. The head of Dow's Chilean operations argued successfully that Dow should remain in Chile as long as possible. He pointed out that Dow had put only $6 million in cash into the venture and had raised the rest of its investment through loans guaranteed by the Chilean government. With some luck, he argued, the Petrodow plants could be completed and most of Dow's cash outlays recouped from profits before drastic change occurred. In brief, the decision was "to stay and try to milk the thing for whatever it might be worth."[4]

In April 1971 the Chilean government informed Dow that it wished to renegotiate the Petrodow agreement to increase the government's ownership from 30 to 51 percent. Dow politely rejected the offer, having no intention of altering its policy of avoiding joint ventures in which it did not have management control. Following months of inconclusive negotiations, government-inspired strikes at Dow's facilities, and growing chaos in the Chilean economy and political system, the government seized Dow's properties.

A visit by the president of Dow Latin America with Allende's minister of economics had no results. A Chilean court eventually ruled that the expropriation was illegal, but it had no power to enforce its ruling. Dow reconciled itself to the loss of its properties and turned its attention to collecting on the expropriation insurance it had taken out with OPIC. After Allende's overthrow in September 1973, the new military government invited Dow to return to its operations in Chile. Dow carefully weighed the offer, since accepting it meant the voiding of its insurance claim against OPIC, and decided to return.

Although Dow executives still believe that their original decision to enter Chile was correct, they now give greater weight than before to political factors that bear on their investment decisions.[5] In early 1974 Dow established an ad hoc committee of five or six executives with the task of keeping management alert to any political shifts that could sour potential investment or damage existing ones. This committee seeks to provide the president of Dow Latin America and the board of Dow Chemical with detailed, up-to-date information about the economic, social, and political conditions of every Latin American country in which Dow operates or would like to operate. The committee's reports are drawn from field trips and from interviews with government officials, scholars, and executives of other U.S. companies doing business in the various countries. Dow claims it is simply a coincidence that the reports of the Economic, Social, and Political Committee are referred to by the group's initials— ESP.[6]

Therefore, as a result of its experience, Dow is not only more sensitive to the political pitfalls of its overseas investments, but it is also instituting a more systematic mode of political information gathering and evaluation that goes beyond the mere intuitive judgment of its executives. Although Dow's "ESP" apparently has not brought any sophisticated techniques of political analysis to bear on the measurement of political risk, at the very least it has sought to maximize the use of the available political information in order to estimate the risk more accurately.

MNEs and Political Risk

Not all MNEs have had experiences like Dow's; of those that have, not all have inaugurated explicit procedures for assessing the impact of political factors on investment. Most MNE decision-makers make informed guesses about the likely influence of political factors in the LDCs. They are aware of the fundamental interests that bring MNEs and LDCs together and split them apart. They are sensitive to the fears in the LDCs about the potential for economic, political, and social domination that their investments represent. Yet the task of coping with political considerations that may affect their investment is often difficult for corporate decision makers, because of several underlying conflicts between their corporate objectives and those of the host governments of many LDCs.

The host government of an LDC is usually concerned primarily with economic growth, the mobilization of its population, and political independence. As one author noted, "nationalistic sentiments expressed by a desire for greater economic self-sufficiency frequently inhibit and restrain the operations of multinational firms. . . . This increased concern over foreign economic domination will be the most challenging problem facing the multinational businessman in the 1970's."[7]

In many instances, economic nationalism has grown out of the political nationalism that in many LDCs represents a reaction to the colonial past. Among political elites in many newly independent states, resentment of past economic domination has become distrust of the MNE.

Host countries often treat MNEs involved in extractive industries differently from those engaged in manufacturing—a distinction that has been supported by the United Nations since 1962. Extractive industries cannot relocate as easily as many manufacturing firms can; they must operate where the natural resources exist. But even manufacturing plants may be severely restricted by the costs associated with relocating.

Foreign ownership of natural resources raises serious political, economic, in addition to psychological issues in the host country. The United States has recently begun to feel the uneasiness of foreign investment, such as that of Arab "petrodollars"—despite the difference between ownership and the actual exercise of control. Nevertheless, the major concessions by U.S. MNEs to host country resentment have been to "maintain a low profile, employ local nationals in managerial positions where possible and to otherwise seek to mollify the natives."[8]

A World Bank survey has revealed that in recent years most exploration expenditures have been made in the industrialized countries and that private firms are reluctant to invest in LDCs, primarily because of political risk. For example, U.S. firms prefer to develop a copper deposit with less than one-half percent richness in the United States than deposits that are more than twice as rich in an LDC. Yet the rate of return in minerals projects in LDCs is twice as high as in the industrial countries. For some of the poorest countries in the world, minerals projects may provide the only opportunity for external investment to play a developmental role.[9]

In his analysis of economic nationalism, J. Frederick Truitt distinguishes expropriation from nationalization. Expropriation, he argues, is aimed at a particular company or companies that are taken over by the host government, but nationalization is directed toward a general type of industry or a sector of the economy.[10]

Truitt's analysis indicates that as of the fall of 1970, U.S. and British investors had suffered expropriation and nationalization in Algeria, Argentina, Bolivia, Brazil, Burma, Ceylon, Egypt, India, Indonesia, Iran, Iraq, Libya, Nigeria, Peru, Somalia, South Yemen, Sudan, Syria, Tanzania, and Uganda. His study did not include American and British losses due to the rise of communist regimes in Eastern Europe, Cuba, and China. Taking into account the number of companies expropriated or nationalized as well as the magnitude of the claims that these actions generated, the following countries may be viewed as having dealt particularly harshly with foreign investors: Algeria, Burma, Ceylon, Iraq, Syria, Tanzania, and the United Arab Republic. Truitt cautions, however, that these data may not give an accurate picture to the investor who is interested in future investments in these countries:

> It could well be that nationalization might in some cases be an adjustment in the development process of an emerging nation necessary to shed the last vestige of colonialism and attain some internally defined measure of social justice. In this case the fact that a nation *has* nationalized foreign investment may well indicate that it has wiped the slate clean and settled into a pattern which will permit and encourage negotiated *new* private foreign investment in a new and more stable social and economic contest.[11]

Truitt's data indicate that certain investments have been more susceptible to expropriation and nationalization than others. For both U.S. and British investments following World War II, the service sector—which includes retail trade, commercial banking, export-import trade, and insurance—and the extractive industries have been the most frequent targets of expropriation and nationalization. British losses, occurring mostly in former British colonies, have been especially severe in the insurance and petroleum industries, and Americans have taken the sharpest losses in petroleum, public utilities, and manufacturing. Truitt warns the foreign investor: "One of the critical questions in assessing the risk of expropriation and nationalization is intimately related to the role of private foreign investment in less developed countries: in assessing risk and role it behooves the investor (and students of international business) to bear in mind that the host government will be asking, 'Yes, but what have you done for me lately?' "[12]

American companies that have suffered expropriation and nationalization are generally bitter about the experience and sensitive to the threat. Franklin Root suggests that the typical expropriation experience of an American company follows a definite sequence: warning, management response, compensation offer, management response, and settlement.[13] In Cuba, however, the experience was different. Having chosen to ignore political risk in Cuba, not one U.S. company had taken out AID's investment guarantee insurance to protect its Cuban investments. Castro's nationalization cost U.S. companies an estimated $1.5 billion in assets. Root believes that the lessons of this experience are clear: "International executives are well advised to appraise the risk of expropriation (as well as other political risks) in an explicit, systematic fashion before committing resources to a foreign country. This approach to the problem would not only lessen future losses but also prevent the forfeiture of new investment opportunities because of indiscriminate fears of expropriation."[14]

A number of MNEs have recognized this and have thus developed various methods to reduce their vulnerability to the wide range of risks associated with political actions and changes abroad. These methods extend from such financial tactics as hedging in order to reduce the risks associated with currency devaluation to the implementation of comprehensive foreign investment strategies.[15]

Theodore Moran has described one such comprehensive strategy, which he refers to as the "strategy of protection," adopted by Kennecott Copper Company with regard to its Chilean investment.[16] Kennecott developed this strategy recognizing that it could no longer rely on full and direct support from the

U.S. government to protect its investment. Kennecott sought (1) to expose to the risk of nationalization as little of its own capital as possible, (2) to line up maximum international support for the contingency of nationalization, and (3) to raise as high as possible the cost to Chile of nationalizing Kennecott properties.

The heart of Kennecott's strategy was to line up support in the event of expropriation. Under an AID contract of guarantee against expropriation, Kennecott first insured the amount of the sale for $80 million plus interest. The funds were supplied by Chile but committed to the joint project by Kennecott. On entering into the joint venture with Chile, the Kennecott parent company thus had the U.S. government's guarantee to pay, in case of expropriation, an amount larger than the net worth of Kennecott's total Chilean operations before the reassessment of book value. In addition, Kennecott demanded that the sale amount and the Export-Import Bank loan be unconditionally guaranteed by the Chilean state and be governed by the laws of New York State. In effect, these arrangements meant that Kennecott would have a general legal claim against the Chilean state in any court should its investment be expropriated. They also meant that AID, the Export-Import Bank, and Congress would also feel the effects of any nationalization of Kennecott's operations in Chile: the Export-Import Bank would want its loan repaid by Chile as soon as the Kennecott management contract was broken; AID would seek compensation from Chile to avoid paying the insurance claim; and Kennecott could attempt to mobilize support in Congress for the application of the Hickenlooper Amendment. Thus, the U.S. government would not be able to ignore the harm done to Kennecott's Chilean operations. Kennecott's strategy was to make sure that any threat of nationalization would bring about confrontations between the U.S. and Chilean governments.[17]

Kennecott's "strategy of protection" is but one example of strategies of risk reduction adopted by MNEs. Many MNEs feel that they cannot depend on the effective support of their home governments against expropriation or nationalization, and they have constructed what Moran calls "transnational alliances" within their industries. Such agreements among industry members of different countries are intended to deter nationalization by increasing the potential costs of such action to the host country. Typical steps taken by an MNE might include the use of court actions against the host government in third countries and boycotting agreements on the purchase of products from an expropriated facility.

In many industries, the MNE has available a number of options that significantly change the relationship between it and the LDC. Motivated by risk avoidance rather than profit maximization, it might seek greater vertical integration. In determining the relative strength of the host country vis-à-vis the vertically integrated MNE whose control does not extend to the production stage, Moran observes: "The principle involved in all cases is initially simple: the relative strengths of the economic nationalists or the multinational corporations in the international industry depend upon who controls the stage where the greatest barriers to entry are located."[18]

Thus, for example, the power that would accrue to economic nationalists by the nationalization of farms or plantations would not be substantial because of the relative ease of entry by competition into the production stage. The point of oligopoly control differs among industries. Some industries are susceptible to control at the marketing or final distribution stages, but others, such as aluminum, are controlled at the refining or processing stage. The capital investment necessary to build facilities capable of generating the electric power to refine bauxite, as well as the supporting infrastructure, make it unlikely that Jamaica, for example, will attain what it would consider "autonomy." Countries with such natural resources are in a competitive bargaining position vis-à-vis large, vertically integrated corporations such as Alcoa, but their power base is nonetheless relatively weak because of the large capital outlays required for processing and subsequent control.

Thus, the response of certain vertically integrated MNEs to the threat of nationalization or expropriation is predictable. They will attempt to shift the bulk of the profits generated within the system to a stage over which they have firm control. Then they will attempt to shift the risks and uncertainties in the industry onto the new owners of their former mines, plantations, or factories. LDCs that have been tied into a corporate system that gave them access to large industrial markets could find themselves frozen out and restricted to the role of competing for sales with other producers of raw materials in a highly volatile market.[19]

This does not happen when countries control those stages involving the crucial barriers to entry. For example, petroleum-exporting countries are in positions of strength relative to the multinational oil corporations. Even so, it is in their interest to remain within the international oligopoly, either on their own or in a joint venture with the oil corporations, and to play by the rules of the game. Thus, MNEs are not necessarily helpless in confrontations with economic nationalism in the LDCs. They can substantially raise the costs of nationalization to the host country through a number of techniques, the very availability of which can often serve as an effective deterrent.

LDCs and the Investor

Partly in response to the MNEs' past abuses, host countries and international organizations have begun to view international regulation of the MNEs as necessary and desirable. MNEs have been confronted by a growing body of regulations in both the home and host countries during the last few years. Demands for a "New International Economic Order" by numerous LDCs have included the following points:

1. Each state has the right to regulate and exercise authority over the foreign investment in its territory in accordance with its laws and national policies.
2. Multinational Corporations (MNCs) should not intervene in the internal affairs of a host country.
3. Each state has the right to nationalize, expropriate, or transfer ownership of foreign property.
4. Compensation is to be paid by the expropriating state taking into account its relevant laws and regulations and other circumstances that the state may consider pertinent.
5. All investment controversies will be settled under the laws of the host state and in its courts unless there is prior agreement that other peaceful means be sought.[20]

Recent disclosures by approximately two hundred major U.S.

corporations, primarily of the Fortune 500 variety, indicate that over $300 million in corporate funds have been paid to foreign government officials. The U.S. government as well as various international organizations have become involved in efforts to develop a code of conduct for the MNEs. Such efforts reflect the difficulties inherent in the relations between the MNEs and the host countries. In addition, the differences between the types of host countries (industrialized in contradistinction to developing countries) are manifested in their respective positions toward the restrictions to be placed on the MNEs.

The U.S. government has considered a number of laws to regulate the overseas conduct of U.S.-based MNEs. Its efforts may be characterized as unilateral actions to proscribe and punish certain conduct of MNEs. In addition, several international organizations have sought to arrive at an internationally agreed-upon code of conduct. The United States has taken the position that a voluntary, internationally agreed-upon code can serve as a guide for acceptable behavior by host governments and MNEs. The Organization for Economic Cooperation and Development (OECD) is the only international body that has reached agreement on a code of conduct for investments. This agreement was reached after a year and a half of negotiations and was concluded by the OECD Ministers in June 1976.

The U.S. Congress has considered a bill to curb and eliminate such corporate practices as improper payments to foreign officials. The measure seeks to achieve this goal by requiring U.S.-based MNEs publicly to disclose such activities to the Office of Foreign Business Practices, which would be created within the Department of Commerce.

The Overseas Private Investment Corporation Act of 1978 calls for the termination of OPIC insurance if the MNE has made illegal payments to foreign officials. The Unlawful Corporate Payments Act of 1977 seeks to impose criminal penalties on U.S. corporations that make illegal payments to foreign officials. It provides for the imposition of criminal penalties on corporations as well as on corporate officials. To quote Congressman Eckhardt (D.-Texas): "The bill would prohibit all U.S. corporations and their subsidiaries which are more than 50 percent owned from making payments, promises of payment, or authorization of payment of anything of value to any foreign official, political party, candidate, or intermediary, where there is a corrupt purpose. The corrupt purpose must be to induce the recipient to influence any official act or decision of a government. So-called grease or facilitating payments made to government officials for the performance of ministerial or clerical duties would not be covered by the bill."[21]

U.S. investments have been primarily concentrated in the OECD countries, which account for nearly 80 percent of total world investment and thereby provide a powerful arena for the establishment of a code of conduct. The essential elements of the OECD code of conduct may be summarized as follows:

1. Reaffirmation of a common interest in a liberal international investment climate;
2. Agreement to a norm of national treatment for foreign-owned enterprises;
3. Agreement to take each other's interests into account and consult on incentives and disincentives to avoid beggar-thy-neighbor actions in the investment area;
4. Voluntary guidelines for MNCs operating in their territories embodying what governments collectively consider to be high standards of good business practices; and
5. Establishment of a consultative process [the OECD's Committee on International Investment and Multinational Enterprises carries this out] to review experience under each of the above elements of the investment package.[22]

The major U.S. government effort is in seeking to assure a system for open and free flow of investments. The U.S. government has supported the efforts within the OECD for a number of reasons. For example, the OECD agreement provides standards for nondiscriminatory treatment between local and foreign-owned enterprises. In addition, the U.S. government favors a voluntary code, whereas the developing countries insist on a binding agreement. In short, the OECD agreement embodies the basic U.S. position on a code of conduct, a position that has been summarized as follows:

1. Be voluntary in nature, that is, not constituting legally binding commitments among states or establishing legally

recognized or enforceable rights and duties on states or enterprises.

2. Be appropriately balanced in reference to the responsibilities [contractual obligations freely undertaken] of governments as well as to the responsibilities of multinational business.

3. Not be used as a basis for discriminating against multinational enterprises as opposed to domestic firms, and provide for nondiscriminatory treatment for established multinational enterprises except under specifically defined and limited circumstances.

4. Not derogate from those principles governing the treatment of foreigners and their property rights, which international law embodies.

5. Apply to all enterprises whether they might be privately owned, government owned, or mixed.[23]

One of the major differences between the OECD position and the LDCs' preference is in the role and responsibilities of the host country. The LDCs have thus far opposed efforts to delineate host government responsibilities within the framework of a code of conduct. Yet the clarification of the host countries' role and responsibilities is crucial for the MNE's expectations of host country behavior—for example, in terms of unilateral modification or revocation of contracts. The conflict between the industrialized countries and LDCs is most clearly reflected in UN forums.

The UN Commission on Transnational Corporations has been attempting to develop a code of conduct since 1975. However, the LDCs have insisted that the proposed code place the responsibilities and burdens solely on the MNEs, not on the host country; this insistence has resulted in an inability to reach an agreement. Nevertheless, the UN Declaration on a New International Economic Order and the UN Charter on the Economic Rights and Duties of States adopt a position on sovereignty over natural resources that would allow a host country to modify or revoke contract provisions at will. At more recent meetings of the Commission on Transnational Corporations, no mutually acceptable position could be found to bridge the gap between the industrialized and less developed countries.

The LDCs have slowed down the pace of these negotiations so that the achievement of an illicit payment agreement will not result in the abandonment of a general UN-sponsored code of conduct.

As a general rule, many LDCs do not have a developed legal tradition that seeks to promote competition. Although LDCs wish to control the business practices of corporations operating within their borders, their other objectives regarding Restrictive Business Practices (RBPs) remain unclear. Even though draft texts have been prepared and types of practices have been identified for consideration, there is, as in other areas, substantial disagreement between the industrialized and developing countries on the standards for the reduction or elimination of Restrictive Business Practices.

Some of the key points on which they differ are:

1. The LDCs seek preferential treatment which would have the effect of exempting LDC enterprises and governmental producer cartels from the scope of the principles.
2. The LDCs wish to control the internal activities of corporations, that is, relations between a parent and its subsidiary or affiliate.
3. The LDCs would declare as illegal developed country export cartels [for example, the U.S. Webb-Pomerence Associations].
4. The LDCs seek, as a minimum, a multilateral complaint mechanism within the UNCTAD.
5. The LDCs do not wish any form of extraterritorial applications of laws, except where they may be applied by the host country against its own MNCs.
6. Generally speaking, the LDCs do not base their objectives for control of business practices on the underlying concept of competition.[24]

Formulating a code of conduct for the regulation of the transfer of technology has involved the most difficult negotiations between the industrialized and developing countries (Group of 77). The gap between them remains substantial in terms of both the approach and substance, despite two years of negotiations and a number of proposed drafts by both sides as well as the socialist countries. The LDCs insist that they have an absolute right of access to the technology under favorable terms; the industrialized countries argue, on the other hand, that they have a property right in the technology, which they will transfer only under conditions that are mutually beneficial. In addition, as in the other code negotiations, the LDCs are seeking a binding code; the industrialized countries insist on a voluntary agreement. The United States has taken the position that if the Group of 77 is not willing to compromise its position, the prospects for a code of conduct for technology transfer are extremely bleak.

Viewed from the perspective of the U.S. government, the basic areas of disagreement regarding a code for the transfer of technology are:

1. The deadlock on the legal nature of the code.
2. The Group of 77 insists that technology is the "universal heritage of mankind" and therefore access to it is an absolute right. [The industrialized countries assert] that access to technology can only be facilitated under mutually advantageous terms and conditions. The Group of 77 will not accept this concept nor will they agree that "mutual benefits must accrue to technology suppliers and recipients in order to maintain and increase the international flow of technology."
3. The Group of 77 insists that the code of conduct be the basis for the negotiation of transfer of technology transactions. [The industrialized countries are] opposed to this concept.
4. The Group of 77 places great emphasis on a chapter entitled Guarantees, under which the parties to technology transfer transactions would guarantee certain performance factors such as levels of production, use of local personnel, export performance, use of local materials, appropriateness of the technology, etc. [The industrialized countries are] opposed to this approach and [stress] general responsibilities of enterprises.
5. [The industrialized contries support] sanctity of contracts and respect for industrial property. The Group of 77 will not accept these concepts.

6. The Group of 77 has a chapter on national regulation which, based on the right of sovereign states to adopt laws and regulations, lists several types of laws for which they seek [the industrialized countries'] endorsement (e.g., laws on renegotiation of contracts, regulation of terms and conditions, special treatment for recipient enterprises, etc.). [The industrialized countries] cannot agree to this approach.

7. [The industrialized countries insist] on mention of respect for international law and treaties. The Group of 77 rejects this principle.

8. The Group of 77 requires outright prohibition of some 40 business practices. [The industrialized countries support] restrictive business practice standards based on a rule of reason concept. Some progress was made in this area, but there remains a wide area of disagreement around all of the practices.

9. In a section of special treatment for developing countries, the Group of 77 positions in areas such as taxation, credit, etc. are not acceptable.

10. The Group of 77 insists that the law of the recipient country will apply exclusively. [The industrialized countries] cannot accept this concept.[25]

Negotiations over the adoption of a code of conduct have manifested fundamental disagreements between the industrialized and developing countries. The proper obligation of the host country vis-à-vis the MNE remains the most serious obstacle to the development of a code of conduct for both investments and transfer of technology. The MNEs feel that LDCs should (1) provide stability for their investments, (2) not discriminate against foreign investments, and (3) honor agreements. But the LDCs have shown little inclination to compromise their positions regarding such matters as the host country's right to revoke a contract unilaterally. The current lack of balance between the responsibilities and obligations that the LDC-sponsored codes of conduct place on the MNEs in comparison to the host countries makes the prospects for a comprehensive agreement unlikely. The establishment of reciprocal obligations of the host country and the MNE must provide, from the perspective of the MNEs, for the stability and integrity for investments and contracts between the MNEs and LDCs. However, agreements on specific aspects of MNE regulation, such as the bribery issue, are more likely to be achieved. Whether the LDCs will agree to voluntary codes on specific issues rather than a binding, comprehensive code remains unclear.

Despite the problems encountered in the negotiations between the industrialized and developing countries regarding a code of conduct, both the U.S. government and U.S.-based MNEs have taken steps to cope with the issue of the conduct of U.S. foreign investment. The U.S. government is now considering the legislation described above. Furthermore, many U.S.-based MNEs have formulated and adopted codes of conduct for their employees. Accordingly, it is relatively easy to observe several limitations that have been imposed on the conduct of U.S.-based MNEs. However, it is much more difficult to assess the degree to which these measures have in fact restricted the MNEs.

In the last decade, the LDCs have been increasingly successful in their efforts to maximize their benefits and minimize their costs from foreign investments. Many are now forming more realistic national economic policies and exercising greater control over their national finances. Fred Bergsten suggests that most host countries have begun to adopt "a pragmatic approach" to foreign investments because of their strong need for capital, technology, and managerial skills.[26] There are good reasons for this "pragmatic approach."

During the global recession of the mid-1970s, many LDCs found themselves in an increasingly difficult economic and political predicament. The dramatic increase in the price of oil and the decline in the price of many of the raw materials and other products exported by many LDCs have exacerbated the already serious issue of how these countries will finance their current imports and buy those capital goods that are critical for economic growth.

The total debt incurred by the LDCs in 1976 reached $145 billion, which represents a dramatic increase from the $70 billion debt incurred as of the end of 1973. Foreign governments' development assistance has aided some LDCs. In 1975 this aid amounted to $17 billion, with the oil-rich countries providing approximately $3 billion of the total.

Private capital markets have begun to play an increasingly important role in the financing and development of many LDCs.[27] By 1976 private money markets provided almost 50 percent of the annual credit flow to the LDCs. Consequently, the LDCs have had to use much of their foreign exchange in order to service their debt. In fact, the interest portion of the debt had increased to 45 percent by 1976. Therefore, most, if not all, LDCs still have substantial problems in the area of capital formation.

Notwithstanding these facts, many LDCs have developed strategies to deal more effectively with foreign investors. As they have become aware of the similarity of many of their national, social, and economic goals, they have begun to cooperate in promoting their common interests. At the same time, the ability of MNEs to influence host country policies has generally been on the wane. Although this is more true of extractive than of manufacturing and service industries, the overall trend nevertheless points to growing bargaining leverage by the host countries. Some still ascribe great power to the MNEs; for example, Barnet and Müller maintain that "the men who run the global corporations are the first in history with the organization, technology, money, and ideology to make a credible try at managing the world as an integrated unit."[28] But the actions that host countries have been able to take against MNEs suggest that the MNEs' "omnipotence" is more illusory than real. This is not to suggest that those who argue the other extreme—namely, that the MNEs have no power—are any more accurate.

Although in the past host countries seeking to control external investors had few policy options short of expropriation and petty harassment, they now have a much wider array of choices. Indeed, in many LDCs, straightforward expropriation is rapidly being overshadowed by "domestication" strategies. Expropriation means that the host government arbitrarily sets the price it will pay for the ownership of a company, ownership that it has established by decree. Domestication, on the other hand, means pressure by the host government on the foreign-owned enterprise to surrender various measures of ownership and control. The host government may apply this pressure by enacting laws that cause

sundry difficulties for the foreign-owned enterprise in its
operations.

For example, Revere Copper and Brass has asserted a claim of
over $90 million against OPIC under expropriation coverage of
its bauxite and alumina facilities in Jamaica. It claims that such
steps as the bauxite production levy that have been taken by the
government of Jamaica are in effect expropriatory. OPIC has
rejected the claim by arguing that the facilities have not been
nationalized and that Revere's problems are commercial in
nature. The case is now in arbitration.

Domestication involves the transfer of control of a foreign
enterprise or investment to the host country's nationals. A host
country's general policy may be to align the enterprise's activities
with those of the government's declared national interests.
Among the specific measures and regulations a host country may
implement are installment of more nationals vested with greater
decision-making powers in higher-level management positions,
transfer of partial ownership to nationals, and implementation of
export quotas.[29]

Thus, in Peru, a new industrial law requires that in the next ten
years the government buy over two-thirds control of all the basic
industries in order to sell the equity to Peruvian nationals. Those
foreign investors in other industries will have to sell majority
control to Peruvian nationals within a short time and will be
limited in each industry to 25 percent ownership. The employees
will eventually become the majority owners as each company will
be obligated to reinvest 15 percent of its annual net profits into
company shares for the employees up to the 51 percent figure.

The host government that seeks to domesticate rather than
expropriate is seeking the best of both worlds. If it expropriates or
nationalizes a foreign-owned enterprise, it often loses the
corporation's managerial expertise and marketing infrastructure.
As a result, the nationalized capital investment may well be
rendered worthless. If it has a successful domestication policy, on
the other hand, the foreign corporation will keep its interest in the
well-being of its operation. However, when an MNE must, by
government decree, sell a percentage of its ownership within a
certain time, it will get a price that will be only part of the actual
value of its investment. To avoid this contingency, some observers

have proposed MNEs should adopt a strategy of predetermined domestication.

A predetermined domestication strategy would seek to preempt a more costly domestication policy imposed by a host country. By selling equity to nationals and involving nationals in the management of the enterprise, an MNE might hope to avert more sweeping and enforced measures by the host government. In 1967, following substantial pressure from the Chilean government, Kennecott negotiated a contract whereby the government of Chile held 51 percent of the shares. Nevertheless, Kennecott retained effective control. The disadvantage of such a strategy is that it may lead to pressures from other host countries where the firm has operations. Additional corporate steps could feature integrating the local companies into worldwide marketing programs and attempting to establish the enterprise without requesting special concessions from the host government. Such corporate strategies may have limited effectiveness in certain countries with respect to particular enterprises. Yet they cannot cope with the full array of risks facing MNEs, let alone balance the fundamental shifts in bargaining power in favor of host countries.

The United States and MNE-LDC Relations

There has recently been much debate on the role of the MNEs. Many observers have concluded that the size, power, and foreign ownership of the MNEs must bring them into conflict with the policies of the nation-state. The American MNE is considered to have a strong influence on U.S. foreign policy. Some even suggest that the major determinant of U.S. foreign policy is the country's foreign investment exposure.[30] Some observers regard the MNE as a beneficial entity for transcending nationalism and improving the lot of mankind; others consider it a tool for perpetuating the division between rich and poor at both the individual and nation-state levels.[31]

Between 1966 and 1975, U.S. direct investment in the developing countries rose from $13.9 billion to $34.9 billion. By comparison, however, U.S. investment in the industrialized countries amounted to about $101 billion in 1976.[32] The rise in investments in LDCs represented a 151 percent increase, which was roughly equivalent to the 158 percent rise in U.S. investments in the industrialized countries. Much of the increased investment in the LDCs, however, was concentrated in a few selected countries. Brazil with $3.7 billion and Mexico with $1.8 billion in foreign investments accounted for $5.5 billion, or about 26 percent, of the total increase of $21 billion. U.S. direct investment more than doubled in Mexico and increased more than an incredible 400 percent in Brazil during the period.[33] Only relatively small amounts of U.S. investment flowed into those other LDCs that are, in fact, in greatest need of external stimuli. Because of this, such critics of OPIC as Senator Church (D.-Idaho) point out that it is the MNE that makes the decision where it will invest its resources and that OPIC insurance merely follows these investments. Even OPIC's president has admitted that the investment is made by the investor, with OPIC playing only a secondary role. Since MNEs invest abroad only if they can make a profit, according to Senator Church, they do not need OPIC-type incentives.

As LDCs and U.S.-based MNEs negotiate over a wide range of critical economic issues, the U.S. government appears to be merely an interested bystander. Although such negotiations increasingly affect U.S. national interests, the U.S. government—unlike those of Great Britain, France, Sweden, Japan, Germany, and others—does not generally get actively involved. It was once commonly assumed that U.S. firms could be counted on to represent U.S. national interests explicitly, or at least to advance them inadvertently. Today, however, many firms that were once U.S.-based have become truly multinational, and they pursue interests that may diverge widely from U.S. national interests.[34] In addition, host country requirements for investment may also seriously affect U.S. national interests.

This development is of considerable importance at a time when the United States is increasingly dependent on the LDCs for various natural resources. The LDCs endowed with those natural resources that the United States must import in large amounts may well find themselves with a near monopoly; they may then demand higher prices for these resources as well as the right and facilities to process and market these resources themselves. The oil-producing countries have already begun colluding with

MNEs, and LDCs with other natural resources could well emulate them.

Copper, tin, natural rubber, and bauxite are some of the natural resources whose supply is dominated by as few as four countries. The four countries that control over 80 percent of the world's exportable supply of copper have begun to organize. Yet the current low price of copper prevents them from exerting substantial pressure. The supply of some of these natural resources is crucial to the well-being of the industrialized countries. As LDCs become more aware of this and recognize the control that a monopolized market may give them, the threat to vital U.S. national interests will mount commensurately.[35]

U.S. national interests in LDCs relate not only to the supply of increasingly scarce raw materials. Much of the U.S. investment in the Third World is in the raw materials sector. Since about 5 percent of U.S. corporate profits are a direct result of this investment, which also provides $1 billion a year for the U.S. balance of payments, acts harmful to these investments are likely to have a serious affect on many U.S. corporations.

The U.S. economy is increasingly vulnerable to world commodity arrangements, the structure of world markets, and changes in exchange rates. The operations of MNEs significantly affect all of these developments. Moreover, the relationships of MNEs to the U.S. economy, particularly with respect to the "export of jobs," are becoming an increasingly volatile domestic issue in the United States itself. In the next chapter, we will discuss some of the aims of U.S. foreign economic policy, with special attention to MNE interactions with the U.S. government and to OPIC's purposes and activities.

The U.S. Government and American Foreign Investment

After World War II, the United States adopted the policy of rebuilding Western Europe and stimulating the flow of private investment. One stimulus was a government insurance program to guarantee private investments against the possibility of the inconvertibility of assets. With the example of the successful Marshall Plan and the need to encourage development in the Third World, Congress in the 1950s shifted the focus of the investment insurance program to the LDCs.

During the 1950s U.S. policymakers viewed the attainment of a certain threshold of economic development as necessary for political stability and the prevention of communist subversion in the LDCs. Although foreign aid was the major instrument used by the United States during the late 1940s and early 1950s to encourage economic development in the LDCs, private U.S. capital was looked upon as the government's logical partner in fostering development and stability. By modifying its investment insurance program to cover U.S. investments in the LDCs, the U.S. government was taking cognizance of the political factors that had previously inhibited U.S. investments in those countries. The general belief was that an investment guarantee program would stimulate the flow of private capital into the LDCs and that U.S. private investment would eventually supplant direct foreign aid.

During the 1960s AID administered the insurance and loan guarantee program. In 1969, Congress established the Overseas Private Investment Corporation (OPIC) and entrusted it with administering the U.S. insurance guarantee program. Ever since

OPIC's inception, there has been conflict as to which of its dual purposes commands priority—whether it is to protect the interests of the U.S. investor or assist the LDCs' economic development. The Foreign Assistance Act of 1969 required OPIC to operate as a nonprofit business enterprise. Section 231 of the act states that OPIC's purpose is "to mobilize and facilitate the participation of United States private capital and skills in the economic and social progress of less developed friendly countries and areas, thereby complementing the development assistance objectives of the United States."

Yet in another paragraph in the same section, OPIC is required both to "conduct its financing operations on a self-sustaining basis" (Section 231a) and to "conduct its insurance operation with due regard to the principles of risk management" (Section 231d). Finally, OPIC is enjoined (Section 231f) to be selective in the projects it insures, such as "to encourage and support only those private investments in less developed friendly countries . . . which are sensitive and responsive to the special needs and requirements of their economies, and which contribute to the social and economic development of their people."

OPIC's multiple purposes have thus made it difficult to evaluate its performance or to weigh the benefits that accrue to the United States from its investment guarantee program. The House and Senate hearings on OPIC in 1973 and 1977 vividly demonstrated both of these difficulties and the efforts made to resolve them. Before looking at some of the issues raised in the hearings, a brief review of OPIC's insurance program, its management policies, and its insurance rates is in order.

The OPIC Insurance Program

Like AID before it, OPIC provides coverage to approved American investors in selected LDCs of up to 90 percent for three types of risk: inconvertibility of assets, war, and expropriation.[1] It provides inconvertibility insurance whereby the investor will receive dollars if the host country's central bank, or its equivalent, refuses to convert locally held funds to dollars. However, it does not cover losses incurred through devaluation of local currencies. Second, OPIC provides war risk insurance, which protects the investor against losses incurred through revolution, insurrection, and war. Since private insurance companies traditionally exclude coverage of war losses, the U.S. government, through a number of different agencies, has provided protection against these losses— for U.S. airlines through the Federal Aviation Administration, for the U.S. merchant fleet through the Maritime Administration, for U.S. exports through the Export-Import Bank, and for foreign investments through OPIC. Finally, OPIC provides insurance coverage against the expropriation of U.S. investments.

As of May 31, 1977, OPIC had an exposure of $2.81 billion in inconvertibility insurance. By 1974 investors had paid $46 million for this coverage, and over $2.1 million had been paid in claims. OPIC's outstanding inconvertibility coverage is concentrated in the chemical, machinery, and manufacturing industries. Lloyd's of London and other London insurers reinsure five percent of OPIC's inconvertibility losses with annual limits of $2 million per country and $6 million in the aggregate.

As of May 31, 1977, OPIC's war risk coverage stood at $2.68 billion. Since the program's beginning, cumulative war risk premium income has been about $89 million. From 1957 through September 1976, nine claims totaling $1 million were paid.

As of May 31, 1977, the expropriation portfolio had an exposure of approximately $3.38 billion, with a portion reinsured. A three-year reinsurance agreement with Lloyd's of London and other London insurers went into effect on January 1, 1977. The agreement provides that the reinsurers cover 62 percent of OPIC's expropriation losses with annual limits of $24.75 million per country and $74.25 million in the aggregate. OPIC's outstanding expropriation coverage is focused on the chemical and mining industries and is largely a carryover from AID's portfolio.

Table 2.1 notes the total current insurance portfolio outstanding by region in 1976 and OPIC's maximum insurance written by region in 1977. Figure 2.1 summarizes OPIC's insurance portfolio by type for the 1969-1974 period. The drop in coverage in 1973 is conspicuous. In 1976 as well as 1977, OPIC again witnessed a substantial decline in its insurance coverage.

Although they are largely a carryover from the AID portfolio, OPIC's current expropriation, war, and inconvertibility exposures are still concentrated in certain countries (See Table 2.2). Figure 2.2 indicates the industry concentration of coverage issued by OPIC and by AID. As a result of OPIC's policies designed to

TABLE 2.1

CURRENT OPIC INSURANCE PORTFOLIO

	Total Current Insurance Portfolio Outstanding by Region in 1976	Maximum Insurance Written by Region in 1977
Latin America	45%	43%
Asia	43%	45%
Africa	11%	10%
Other	1%	2%

Source: Overseas Private Investment Corporation, 1977 Annual Report, p. 13.

limit coverage in industries or projects that are vulnerable or sensitive to political risk, coverage for the extractive industry has been reduced.

OPIC strives to operate on a self-sustaining basis. In 1977 its net income amounted to $47.8 million, and its total insurance and finance reserves increased to a total of $230.1 million and $100 million, respectively. Whether these reserves are sufficient remains unclear because of the danger of catastrophic losses such as those in Chile. For example, in 1971 OPIC's potential liability from claims totaled over $400 million; its reserves were only $85 million. In fact, only in 1977 did OPIC resolve Anaconda's $154 million expropriation claim. A compromise was reached following arbitration, which found OPIC liable. The same process occurred in the ITT Chilean claim. Under the terms of the Anaconda settlement, OPIC agreed to pay Anaconda $47.5 million and received $27.5 million of promissory notes acquired by an Anaconda subsidiary under an agreement reached with Chile in 1974. OPIC also agreed to guarantee the payment of a $47.6 million portion of $188 million in Chilean notes acquired by another Anaconda subsidiary under the same Chilean settlement.

OPIC's Risk Management Policies

Faced with the possibility of catastrophic losses, OPIC has

Figure 2.1
SIX-YEAR SUMMARY OF CURRENT INSURANCE
PORTFOLIO IN BILLIONS OF DOLLARS

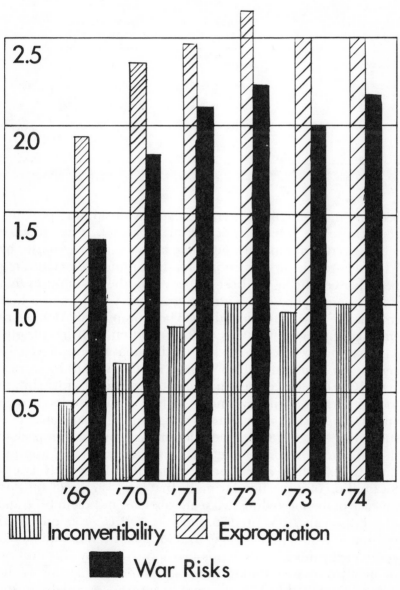

Source: Overseas Private Investment Corporation, 1974 Annual Report, p. 9.

TABLE 2.2

OPIC EXPROPRIATION, WAR AND INCONVERTIBILITY
EXPOSURES BY COUNTRY (TOP FIVE ONLY)

Expropriation Exposure	War Exposure	Inconvertibility Exposure
Jamaica	Jamaica	Brazil
Brazil	Korea	Korea
Korea	Dominican Republic	Dominican Republic
Dominican Republic	Brazil	Philippines
Philippines	Philippines	Indonesia

Source: Overseas Private Investment Corporation, 1977 Annual Report, pp. 12-13.

become increasingly concerned that its insurance program conform to the principles of risk management. It has adopted more selective risk management standards than had been used by AID and provides insurance only for those projects that indicate a probable benefit to the host country—on the assumption that investments compatible with the economic priorities of a host country are less likely than others to be expropriated. As the General Accounting Office (GAO) 1973 report on OPIC points out, AID had not been concerned by the fact that its insurance coverage was concentrated in a few countries and industries.

OPIC's concern with risk management coincided with a shift in focus from AID's primary concern with economic development to added emphasis on making the program financially self-sustaining. The 1978 OPIC legislation may cause a shift back to the original position. While AID's insurance averaged approximately $1.7 billion a year for the period 1966-1970, OPIC issued $1.2 billion of insurance during its first year, 1971, $600 million for each of the succeeding two years, about $1 billion in 1974, and $1.5 billion in 1975. In 1976, however, OPIC wrote only $537 million in insurance coverage. And for the fifteen-month period ending September 30, 1977, it issued approximately $750 million in new insurance. Among the reasons for this decline is the general reduction in U.S. overseas investment, especially in the developing countries. In 1976 total U.S. investment to LDCs fell

Figure 2.2
INDUSTRY CONCENTRATION OF COVERAGE

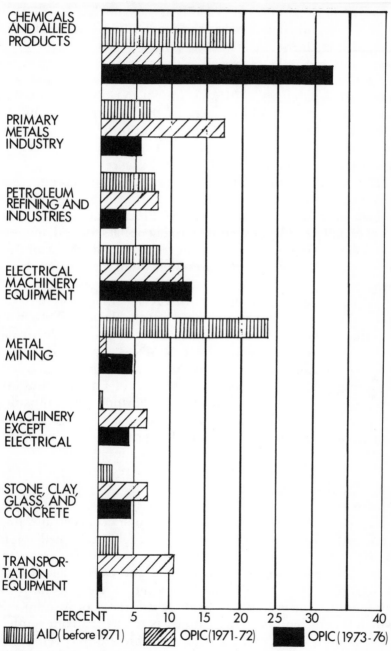

from $7.2 billion in 1975 to $3.3 billion—a trend that continued in 1977. There is also a reduced demand for OPIC insurance once the foreign investment decision has been made. Because of OPIC's premiums and policies as well as their overseas experience, the MNEs are developing their own risk management and self-insurance capabilities. OPIC has sought to embark on a policy designed to reduce the dangers to the investment insurance program associated with high exposure in one country. Catastrophic losses due to massive expropriations in such a country could endanger OPIC's very existence.

The large multinational firms prefer to concentrate their investments in the more developed countries.Very often they do not consider the countries for which OPIC insurance is available to be equally worthy of their investment dollars; indeed, many of the poorer LDCs provide only limited investment opportunities. Thus, the MNEs, not OPIC, direct the flow of U.S. foreign investment dollars. The large MNEs base their investment choice on criteria other than the availability of OPIC insurance and subscribe to a policy because it is available at a reasonable price. Thus, what was intended to be an economic development program has in fact become an insurance service for U.S. MNEs at a cost and under terms that cannot be supplied by the private insurance industry.[2]

During the last four years, 83 percent of OPIC's insurance coverage in dollar terms has been for Fortune 500 companies. Despite OPIC's policy to provide insurance coverage to small firms, the bulk of the demand for political risk insurance nonetheless comes from the large multinationals.

Even though OPIC implemented more restrictive policies on concentration during its first two years of operation, the concentration issue has not been solved. In fact, the GAO report points out that new OPIC insurance is more concentrated than under AID—a concentration that is largely accounted for by Brazil.

In reviewing proposed investments under consideration for insurance contracts, OPIC has taken certain steps to limit the concentration it will allow. In those categories of insurance in which the concentration in a country is greater than one-tenth of the total coverage for that category, the growth in coverage was not to exceed 1 percent of the total OPIC coverage for that category. In 1972 this figure was increased to 2 percent because of the decrease in OPIC's total insurance portfolio.[3]

Even though OPIC still uses the 10 percent guideline, OPIC officials indicate that they will also evaluate the size and nature of the investment as well as the political and economic stability of the host country to determine the appropriate concentration levels. In fact, once a country's concentration reaches 7 percent of OPIC's total portfolio, OPIC will monitor that country in order to diversify and selectively increase its exposure.

OPIC's methods regarding limits on coverage in high-concentration countries have included (1) insuring only partial amounts of investments in such countries and encouraging investments in areas of that country that are not heavily exposed, and (2) requiring large investors desiring OPIC insurance for projects in such countries to share in all losses in excess of $100 million through participation in the Retrospective Premium Adjustment Program. However, because of its complexity and the negative response it evoked from the business community, the Retrospective Premium Adjustment Program was abondoned. In January 1976, OPIC's Board of Directors also authorized the establishment of a War Risk Insurance Reciprocal, whereby the recipients of the coverage collectively shared the liability for one another's risks. In November 1977, with the elimination of the 1974 statutory "privatization" requirement, OPIC terminated this plan.

OPIC's policy is to engage in some form of political risk assessment in selected countries in which its program is administered and where the political environment is likely to have a bearing on the viability of the insurance policy. Although OPIC itself does some of this analysis, it generally follows the analysis and advice of the State Department, with which it has a semiofficial relationship, before deciding to suspend or cease issuing insurance for enterprises in a particular country. As a host government's attitude toward foreign investment becomes more hostile, OPIC usually attempts to monitor the situation closely before taking action. In order not to exacerbate the situation in the host country, OPIC's analyses are often not made public; new insurance contracts are simply not written. OPIC has curtailed its insurance for reasons ranging from a country's suspension of a foreign investor's currency convertibility rights to an already high concentration of OPIC insurance coverage in that country. The existence of a U.S.-based company's claim against OPIC's insurance program is not considered a proper reason for suspending the insurance program in that country. Moreover, OPIC does recognize the right of a host government to expropriate foreign investments. However, such expropriations are considered improper only when just compensation is not provided.

Under section 231(1) of the Foreign Assistance Act of 1961, as amended by the OPIC Amendments Act of 1974, OPIC is required, to the extent practicable, to give preferential consideration to projects in the LDCs whose per capita income is $450 or less (1973 U.S. dollars). Nevertheless, OPIC was not successful in shifting insurance coverage to the poorer countries. Largely as a result of the 1977 congressional hearings, OPIC's Board of Directors decided to restrict OPIC's programs in developing countries with incomes over $1,000 per capita[4] (1975 dollars) and provide special attention to projects in countries with a GNP of less than $520 per capita (1975 dollars). In these countries, U.S. private investment projects that satisfy OPIC's other criteria will be insured or financed if they are sponsored by U.S. small businesses, are for minerals exploration or development, or involve energy development in non-OPEC (Organization of Petroleum Exporting Countries) states. The board retained a substantial degree of discretion by stating that it will consider, on a case-by-case basis, other projects offering "exceptionally significant developmental benefits" in these countries.[5] Even though OPIC's recent policies are ostensibly aimed at increasing U.S. investment in the poorer LDCs, there is a serious question whether U.S. businessmen will invest in these LDCs. Since most U.S. corporations are primarily interested in such factors as the country's market size, infrastructure, and resources, the availability of OPIC insurance coverage is unlikely to be a critical factor in the investment decision. However, for small U.S. investors as well as for those that seek resources available in a limited number of the poorer LDCs, the availability of OPIC insurance may be the key variable in the company's foreign investment decision strategy. For example, the small U.S. investor may decide to invest in a poorer LDC if OPIC insurance is available when it otherwise would not have done so because of concern or unfamiliarity with the political situation in the host country. An extractive company may be influenced by the availability of OPIC insurance in a host country rich in the particular natural resource. In other words, were such insurance not available, that company would very likely prefer to operate in a "politically safer" environment even if the natural resource is more expensive to extract.

Insurance Rates

Given OPIC's purposes and the nature of the risks for which it writes insurance, the establishment of an appropriate insurance premium has been difficult. This is true both because of the rates established by insurance programs of other countries and because of AID's rates during the Investment Insurance Program's first fifteen years.

OPIC has emphasized the "competition" it faces from the agencies of other countries that offer similar insurance coverage at lower rates. Although the United States was the first to introduce an investment insurance program, fifteen other countries have copied it in various ways.[6] The insurance rates established by developed states range from 0 for Portugal to 1.25 percent for Switzerland. It would appear from such rates that insurance programs are in fact used to subsidize corporate investment abroad. France and Japan have recently expanded their insurance programs, apparently to secure foreign sources of raw materials.

OPIC's pre-1978 insurance rate structure was influenced to a considerable degree by AID's experience in dealing with insurance claims. AID had virtually no significant insurance claims during its fifteen-year management of the insurance program; premiums over this period were reduced by nearly two-thirds from the maximum of 4 percent annually. Those rates were, of course, not based on any scientific or actuarial criteria, nor were OPIC's readjustments of these rates before 1978 based on the size of its claims during that period. Though not drastic, OPIC's rate increase from 1.125 percent to 1.5 percent annually for full coverage represented, when coupled with changes in the length and scope of newly written OPIC insurance, a significant change in the program's premium structure.

Many suggestions have been made for changing OPIC's premium rate structure. Keith Wheelock has suggested that "while a ranking of political risk by country is neither desirable nor technically feasible, a staggered fee schedule can be established in various sectors such as mining, manufacturing, turnkey operations, and management services which would include some capital investment. This could permit flexibility to encourage new modes of investment."[7]

An annual risk-ranking of countries would be exceedingly difficult for OPIC to develop, given the criteria it would likely be based on. Moreover, publication of such a ranking would probably strain relations between those countries with a high-risk rating and the U.S. government. Accordingly, OPIC has not sought to set rate premiums based on political criteria. In 1978, however, it did adopt base rate premiums for different industries. These rates may be increased or decreased by up to one-third depending on the risk profile of the particular project. These base rates are presented in Table 2.3.

There is no precise method to measure the inducement provided by the availability of OPIC insurance at a given rate to a proposed overseas investment by a U.S. corporation. In many cases, however, the corporation apparently proceeds with its investment regardless of the availability of OPIC insurance, at whatever premium is involved. In many cases, OPIC's insurance has been sought because of its easy availability and relatively low cost. However, for some investors the availability of OPIC insurance has been crucial. For some small corporations, the very *possibility* of a loss is sufficient to inhibit foreign investment. The Congressional Research Service of the Library of Congress has estimated that between 10 to 20 percent of U.S. companies' nonpetroleum investments in developing countries would not have been made in the absence of OPIC insurance.

The 1973 Congressional Hearings

The contrast between the 1973 Senate and House subcommittee hearings on OPIC was marked. The two bills in question (S. 2957 and H.R. 13973), the number and type of witnesses called, and the

TABLE 2.3

OPIC's 1978 PREMIUMS

I. Manufacturing/Service Projects Coverage	Current(%)	Stand-by(%)
Inconvertibility	.30	.25
Expropriation	.60	.25
War, Rev., Insurr.	.60	.25

II. Natural Resources Projects (other than Oil and Gas) Coverage	Current(%)	Stand-by(%)
Inconvertibility	.30	.25
Expropriation	.90	.25
War, Rev., Insurr.	.60	.25

III. Oil and Gas Projects Coverage	Exploration(%)	Production(%)
Current Comprehensive	1.30	2.80
Primary Stand-by	.30	.75
Secondary Stand-by	.03	.03

IV. Institutional Loans Coverage	Current(%)	Unused Commitment(%)
Inconvertibility	.25	.20
Expropriation	.30	.20
War, Rev., Insurr.	.60	.20

V. Service Contractors Coverage	Current(%)	Stand-by(%)
Inconvertibility	.30	.25
Expropriation	.60	.25
War, Rev., Insurr.	.60	.25
Non-payment/Disputes	.80	.25
Performance Bonds, Letters of Credit	.50	--

tenor of the questions directed to these witnesses revealed the Senate subcommittee's basic hostility to, and the House subcommittee's basic sympathy with, OPIC. Taken together, the two sets of hearings provided a searching review of OPIC's successes and failures. The brief discussions of the Senate and House hearings that follow illustrate not only their basic differences in perspectives but also their differing conclusions, especially regarding OPIC's purposes.

The Senate Subcommittee on Multinational Corporations, chaired by Senator Frank Church (D.-Idaho), seriously questioned the developmental role of OPIC's investment insurance program. It pointed to the large percentage increase of new investments in the LDCs and the rising percentage of uninsured investments as indications that the availability of insurance has little impact on the flow of private capital to the LDCs. The Senate also noted that the OPIC-insured investments have been concentrated in but a few LDCs. Eight countries accounted for 83 percent of OPIC's insured investments, and over one-half of OPIC's insurance was in just three countries—Korea, Indonesia, and Brazil.[8] The Senate subcommittee concluded that multinational corporations appear to be interested in investing in only a few selected LDCs.

The House Subcommittee on Foreign Economic Policy, under the leadership of Congressman John Culver (D.-Iowa), interpreted these statistics differently. Based on the testimony of OPIC's management as well as other witnesses sympathetic to OPIC, it concluded that OPIC had not had sufficient time to publicize the availability of its insurance for many underdeveloped countries. It agreed with OPIC that the concentration of investment in a handful of countries would be eliminated if OPIC had the opportunity to develop its "catalytic" role. With insurance available, the investor might go into one of the least developed countries, even if foreign investment laws were unsettled and socioeconomic and political trends unstable. Thus, the House subcommittee, arguing that it was only a matter of time until OPIC fulfills its development role and lessens the concentration of its coverage, concluded that OPIC's authorization should be extended to give it an opportunity to implement its mandate.

The Senate Subcommittee on Multinational Corporations held that the availability of OPIC insurance did not seem to affect the basic investment decision. Once they decide to invest, it argued, MNEs insure their investments if the premium rates are low enough to make purchase attractive for the risks they fear exist.[9] The Senate subcommittee suggested that OPIC primarily benefited the U.S. investor and not the developing countries. It reported that OPIC was apparently unable to persuade MNEs to invest in most of the poorer countries, and it concluded that OPIC's insurance program could not be justified on the basis of the aid it provided to the development of the LDCs: "Rather, the program is used by American corporations as an insurance program which lowers their risk against adverse political events in less developed countries. If the program is to be continued it should conform to the rationale for which it is used, an insurance program and not a development aid program."[10]

The House subcommittee came to different conclusions. It noted that OPIC can and should play a positive development role in directing the forms of U.S. investment. Moreover, contrary to the Senate's suggestion that MNEs insure foreign investments only if the premium is attractive, OPIC suggested to the House that MNEs often will not even invest unless insurance is available. Even for those investors that do not purchase insurance because of its cost, the fact that OPIC is willing to insure an investment suggests a minimal level of security against political risks. OPIC further argued that the absence of investments in many of the poorer countries was not due to failure in its program but simply to ordinary business economics. In short, there simply are not any economical, viable investments to be made in some countries.

In addition to its concern over the purpose of OPIC's insurance program, the Senate subcommittee was troubled that the insurance program promoted confrontations between the U.S. government and host governments. The subcommittee, though recognizing that OPIC's quasi-governmental character often allows it to serve as an intermediary among the MNE, the LDC, and the U.S. government, suggested that OPIC remains fundamentally linked to the U.S. government, in large part because the U.S. Treasury stands behind OPIC's investment insurance program. In light of OPIC's reserves in relation to its exposure and possibility of catastrophic loss, the U.S. government stands, in fact, as the underwriter of OPIC's potential losses. Thus, the U.S. government has cause for concern over the policies and measures taken by a host country toward a U.S. firm's investment that is covered by OPIC.[11]

On this issue the House subcommittee found that OPIC actually minimizes confrontations between governments by serving as a buffer between the U.S. government and the private investor on the one hand and the host country on the other. It argued that in negotiating claims, OPIC was clearly the government organization most qualified to deal with foreign countries. Moreover, it argued, OPIC is so expert in avoiding intergovernment confrontations over U.S. corporate investments that its role should be expanded so that it participates in every expropriation or nationalization negotiation between a U.S. corporation—OPIC-insured or not—and a foreign country.[12] The House also recommended that the Hickenlooper and Gonzalez amendments, which provide for automatic retaliation by the U.S. government if U.S. assets are expropriated without just compensation, give way to a more flexible system of dealing with expropriations through the OPIC network.

OPIC supported the House sentiments. It argued that it had sought to use alternative methods of settling investment disputes and that it had minimized government-to-government confrontations concerning host government actions: "Probably the most important dimension established in OPIC's first two years, and one still growing in significance, is the constructive role it plays in the avoidance of government-to-government confrontations in investment disputes."[13]

Those investors not insured by OPIC, it was argued, have sought to involve the State Department in their disputes and to have the Hickenlooper and Gonzalez amendments invoked. OPIC noted that those investors it insures who file claims must follow specific procedures involving stages of negotiations with the host government in order to be able to collect on the claim. Under OPIC's insurance scheme, moreover, the insured investor has an incentive to come to terms with the host government, since the political risk insurance does not cover the company's total exposure and loss. Under the terms of the contract an investor makes with OPIC, the investor must attempt to adjudicate the case in the host country's courts for at least a year before the claim against OPIC becomes valid. The danger of immediate government-to-government confrontation is thereby reduced.

The House subcommittee recognized the desirability of eliminating all connections between the U.S. Treasury and OPIC. Instead of scrapping the OPIC program, however, it recommended that OPIC move toward reducing the possibility of catastrophic losses both by diversifying its portfolio and by forming joint ventures with private insurance firms to spread a substantial portion of its political risk exposure.

The Senate subcommittee asserted that because U.S.-based MNEs have used OPIC for their own economic purposes, the U.S. government has on occasion become more involved in the internal affairs of a host country than it otherwise would have. Because of this corporate dependence on the U.S. government, the enterprise may in fact not take preventive measures that could minimize its losses.[14]

OPIC pointed to examples of the contrary. ITT's activities in Chile, it contended, demonstrated that corporations may become involved in the internal affairs of other sovereign countries precisely because they are not insured by OPIC. A large percentage of ITT's investment in Chile was uninsured.

Those who took part in the congressional debates over OPIC generally remained divided between those who saw it primarily as a development aid to the LDCs and those who saw it as a means of protecting the U.S. overseas investor. The key issue remains whether these two goals are compatible.

Recently, some observers have argued that with the increased U.S. dependence on the raw materials found in the LDCs, U.S.-based MNEs should be encouraged to search for, and secure access to, raw materials in order to assure their steady supply. Moreover, many contend that investment guarantees should be offered to extractive industries to encourage foreign production, whether or not the investments are wholly consistent with U.S. foreign policy and economic development goals.

On the basis of OPIC's current insurance portfolio, the Senate subcommittee argued that OPIC has not, in fact, been encouraging this effort to secure raw materials in the LDCs. It pointed out that OPIC has insured very few investments in the metal-mining sector—in contrast to AID, which had about one-fourth of its insurance portfolio in the mining sector. Contrary to OPIC declarations that it was assuring a constant flow of raw materials to the U.S. market, the subcommittee concluded that OPIC had adopted risk management principles that stifled insurance for mining investments: "OPIC cannot argue, on the one hand, that they are minimizing risks and, therefore, not insuring projects in high risk sectors, such as metal mining, and, on the other hand, argue that the investment guarantee program is essential to assure the United States of a source of raw materials."[15]

Once again, OPIC itself saw the case quite differently. It claimed that its risk management principles were not intended to eliminate writing insurance for sensitive extractive industries; rather, they were intended to lower the amount of available coverage while still insuring a large enough percentage to assure that a particular project could be undertaken. OPIC further argued that frequently only 50 to 75 percent of a total investment needs to be insured before an enterprise will invest in a particular extractive project, while other proposed investments may require that 90 to 100 percent coverage be made available. OPIC indicated that contrary to Senate reports, it had never turned down an investment in the mining sector.

The House subcommittee, though not addressing this point specifically, suggested that many alternative arrangements for OPIC programs could eliminate the problems caused in sensitive investment areas. It suggested, for example, that OPIC encourage different types of investments—such as joint ventures, phase-out programs, and nonequity investments—to minimize the hostility that often accompanies investments in important extractive industries.

The House subcommittee made a number of recommendations: for example, that OPIC cooperate more with private insurers, encourage new forms of investment, and make its services more available to both noninsured corporations and smaller businesses. But it generally recommended that the OPIC framework remain intact. The bill that Congress ultimately passed incorporated more of the House subcommittee recommendations than those of the more critical Senate subcommittee.

OPIC, the Insurance Industry, and "Privatization"

One of the prerequisites of writing risk insurance is knowing that the risk in question is insurable—that is, that the probability of loss can be estimated, the appropriate premiums calculated, and reserves accumulated. Avoiding catastrophic loss requires reserves sufficient to cover such occurrences. Without such reserves the insurer must obtain a reinsurer to cover the possibility of catastrophic loss. Because of the lack of information available on the phenomenon and the difficulty of establishing an actuarial-based calculation of the reserve size, political risk cannot, in the ordinary sense, be considered insurable. In part, this is why insurance companies have not directly issued political risk insurance in the past.

Another reason for the insurance companies' hesitation to insure involves their need for evidence that political risk insurance will sell. If only parties facing dangerous risks buy such insurance, there is only a disincentive for an insurance company to offer it. A comparison between earthquake or flood insurance and political risk insurance is enlightening. Earthquakes and floods are common only in certain areas, and when they occur they tend to cause catastrophic losses. If an insurance company offered earthquake or flood insurance alone,[16] then probably only people living in those areas susceptible to earthquakes or floods would purchase it. Clearly, either the insurance company would absorb a loss in this situation or its premiums would be extremely high to protect against catastrophic losses. High premium rates, in turn, would decrease the number of potential purchasers. However, if everybody, including those living in areas not likely to be affected, purchased earthquake or flood insurance, the insurance company would be able both to lower its premiums and to provide coverage for those living in the susceptible high-risk areas.

Similarly, if only those industries that involve a high degree of political risk and those investments in "high-risk" countries are interested in purchasing political risk insurance, then either the insurer will absorb potentially catastrophic losses or else the premium will be extremely high and the number of potential purchasers very low. The theoretical solution is for everyone to purchase such insurance in order to pool the risks. However, just as those who do not perceive danger from floods or earthquakes will not purchase flood or earthquake insurance, those who do not perceive danger from political factors are unlikely to purchase political risk insurance.

The fact that American insurance companies have had no substantial experience in writing political risk insurance has tempered their desire to associate with OPIC. Over the past several years the American insurance industry has become aware that OPIC was and still is overexposed in certain countries, concentrated in similar kinds of investments and in certain types of insurance. The industry's caution is thus understandable.

The Overseas Private Investment Corporation Amendments Act of 1974

During the 1973 Senate and House hearings, OPIC and the GAO provided Congress with reports on OPIC's insurance activities. As a result of these hearings, Congress passed Public Law 93-390, the Overseas Private Investment Corporation Amendments Act of 1974, which makes clear the congressional intent concerning the role of the private insurance industry.

In its report to Congress on the possibility of transferring its programs to the private sector, OPIC described itself as a corporation operating within the U.S. government as "an income-earning insurance service and a commercial term investment finance service for U.S. private investors going into developing countries."[17] Pursuant to its originating legislation[18] requiring it to submit to Congress an analysis of the possibility of transferring all or part of its activities to private associations, OPIC had explored ways of securing greater private participation in its activities without sacrificing its public purposes. It reported to the Congress that it had encountered many difficulties in securing private participation as part of a balanced approach that would (1) serve the developmental purposes for which OPIC was established, (2) protect the U.S. government's financial and foreign policy interests, (3) attract significant private participation, and (4) meet the needs of U.S. investors. OPIC stated that it preferred to test in actual operation various modes of private participation but that it did not have the legal authority to experiment.

OPIC's summary conclusions regarding the possibilities of transferring some of its programs to the private sector were as follows:

1. There are realistic possibilities of inducing significant participation by private insurers, reinsurers, or mutually insuring investors in the investment insurance program. . . .

A set of experimental public-private collaborations should be undertaken before deciding what should be the U.S. Government's long-term role in overseas investment insurance operations.

2. OPIC needs additional statutory authority and time to test various combinations of joint insurance underwriting and reinsurance arrangements with private insurance companies, international agencies and others. . . .

3. Private participation in the form of OPIC's purchase of reinsurance from syndicates of Lloyd's of London, initiated in January 1972 has proved capable of expansion to relieve OPIC of a substantial portion of its liabilities on expropriation insurance. . . . Private reinsurance of OPIC does not, however, provide a full test of the feasibility of transferring direct underwriting responsibilities and claims management in overseas investment insurance to the private sector or sharing these responsibilities and related financial liabilities between the Government and private insurers.

4. The private insurance industry operates under regulations which limit its capacity to cover U.S. overseas investment against political risks. Consequently the industry will not accept large exposure in the unfamiliar field of political risk insurance unless the U.S. Government provides reinsurance against large losses disproportionate to annual premium income. Alternative forms of private underwriting, such as a mutual association of investors, also will require substantial U.S. Government reinsurance. Private insurance companies also will not commit themselves to exposure over an extended term of years in this unfamiliar field.[19]

In short, even though OPIC concluded that attracting significant participation by the private insurance industry was a realistic possibility, the qualifications contained in its report point to its own doubts about reaching the goal. OPIC noted that its insurance program had been examined by insurance actuaries, who agreed that mathematical projections by loss rates cannot be generated on the basis of past experience. Notwithstanding their fifteen years of providing insurance for U.S.-based companies investing in developing countries, neither OPIC nor the AID insurance program had provided sufficient data for the formulation of actuarial projections of future losses: "In summary, the nature of OPIC's investment insurance 'business'—its policy mandates and restrictions, the difficulty of projecting its long-term income, loss ratios, and the potential for catastrophic losses—set real limits on the extent of its transfer to the private sector."[20]

Although OPIC's request for an extension of its mandate generally met with sympathy from the House Subcommittee on Foreign Economic Policy, in its final report the subcommittee made the following recommendations:

> . . . In order to further insulate the U.S. Government from the possibility of a confrontation with a foreign country over investment disputes, and further reduce the risk of loss to the U.S. Treasury, OPIC should pursue its efforts to form with the private insurance industry a joint investment insurance association.
>
> OPIC should eventually be phased down to a minority participant in the association, but the corporation should continue to act as the reinsurer of the association's portfolio. OPIC should use its leverage as a member of the association and as the reinsurer to influence the private insurance companies in the orientation and form of investments insured so that the investments are structured to maximize acceptability to the host country and minimize the risk of expropriation. In addition, OPIC should through its leverage, continue to play a constructive role in the settlement of investment disputes.[21]

As for OPIC's relations with the private insurance industry, the Senate's OPIC bill would have prohibited OPIC from participating in policies for inconvertibility and expropriation risks after December 31, 1979, and for war risks after December 31, 1980. It would also have prohibited OPIC from entering into contracts assuming liability for a private company's policy after January 1, 1978, and required OPIC to act only as a reinsurer after December 31, 1980. Finally, the Senate bill would have extended OPIC's authority for investment insurance only until December 31, 1976.

But, as noted earlier, the bill that emerged from the House-Senate Conference Committee and that became the Overseas Private Investment Corporation Amendments Act of 1974 was far closer to the House than the Senate version.

Its major provisions deal with the "privatization" of some of OPIC's functions.

The 1974 act states the intention of Congress that OPIC achieve the participation of private insurance companies and multilateral organizations in incurring liabilities of risk dealing with expropriation and inconvertibility insurance. For contracts made on or after January 1, 1975, at least 25 percent of this liability should be borne by private insurers, with 50 percent constituting the minimum for contracts issued on or after January 1, 1978. OPIC will no longer be authorized to participate as an insurer of expropriation and inconvertibility insurance contracts issued after December 31, 1979, unless Congress modifies the provision. Moreover, OPIC is to achieve joint participation with the private insurance industry and other insurers incurring liabilities of risk with respect to coverage of war, revolution, and insurrection. For contracts issued on or after January 1, 1976, at least 12.5 percent of the liability should be incurred by the private entities; for those issued on or after January 1, 1979, this liability should be increased to 40 percent.

If OPIC were to find that any of these goals could not be achieved, it had to inform the Senate Committee on Foreign Relations and the House Committee on Foreign Affairs. It had to indicate why it could not achieve the required percentages of participation and to estimate the date by which they can be achieved. For insurance contracts issued after December 31, 1980, OPIC was prohibited from participating as an insurer for risks concerning war, revolution, and insurrection.

By December 31, 1980, OPIC was to become a reinsurer. In short, it would assume limited liability as an insurer for insurance contracts written by private insurance companies. The law stated that

> the amount of reinsurance of liabilities under this title which the corporation [OPIC] may issue shall not exceed $600,000,000 in any one year, and the amount of such reinsurance shall not in the aggregate exceed at any one time an amount equal to the amount authorized for the maximum contingent liability outstanding at any one time under section 235(a) (1). All reinsurance issued by the corporation under this subsection shall require that the reinsured party retain for his own account specified portions of liability,

whether first loss or otherwise, and the corporation shall endeavor to increase such specified portions to the maximum extent possible.[22]

The law also allowed OPIC to request appropriations from Congress should its reserves fall below $25 million. OPIC will be allowed to borrow up to $100 million from the U.S. Treasury in order to meet its insurance and reinsurance liabilities, but it must repay the sum borrowed within one year.

OPIC and Its Dealings with the Private Insurance Industry

Before discussing OPIC's response to the 1974 congressional mandate to phase out over the next six years its direct writing of insurance, we will briefly examine OPIC's past efforts to transfer some of its functions to the private insurance industry. These efforts fall into three general categories: (1) reinsurance, (2) joint underwriting, and (3) parallel underwriting.

Reinsurance

From its inception, OPIC made several efforts to comply with the congressional mandate to transfer its insurance portfolio to the private insurance industry. Contacts were made with U.S insurance and reinsurance companies and with the Lloyd's insurance group of London. The former made no positive response, but a Lloyd's underwriter agreed to form a pool to insure a portion of OPIC's expropriation liabilities.

The Lloyd's agreement of December 1971 constituted the first entry of private insurers into the arena of political risk insurance. It provided that the participating insurers in 1972 be liable for up to $7 million of OPIC's losses on expropriation coverage in all countries except Chile. Consequently, the Lloyd's group liability was 50 percent in those countries where OPIC's total expropriation liabilities amounted to $14 million. OPIC reserved the right to make the decision concerning underwriting policy and claims determination and settlement. The reinsurer had a financing function, received fees, and paid a share of claims as decided by OPIC: "The reinsurer receives 85 percent of the portion of the annual fees collected by OPIC for the current amount of expropriation insurance in each country applicable to the reinsurer's maximum liability."[23]

For 1973 Lloyd's doubled its reinsurance liability in the individual countries to $14 million under the same terms as in the previous agreement. Although OPIC's possible expropriation losses were thus 50 percent reinsured in 80 percent of the countries where OPIC had insurance exposure, this reinsurance agreement did not appreciably alleviate OPIC's possible losses in the event of expropriation in a country such as Jamaica, where OPIC has insured hundreds of millions of dollars worth of investment. However, the interesting point in this reinsurance agreement was the entry of seven U.S. insurance companies into the reinsurance pool.

Lloyd's and the U.S. insurance industry had refused to reinsure OPIC's war and insurrection policies, but they began in 1973 to discuss the feasibility of creating a reinsurance pool for inconvertibility risks. Lloyd's reinsured the expropriation portfolio once again at the end of 1973. OPIC reported to Congress that

> the commitment was made for three years (1974-1976) instead of one year, and Lloyd's per-country liability was increased to $18.25 million. The form of reinsurance was altered from the initial contract-by-contract quota share liability for first losses to an aggregate first-loss pool in which Lloyd's bears slightly more than 45 percent of any OPIC expropriation settlement of up to $40 million in any country (including Chile) per year or up to $120 million globally per year. The method of determining the division of premium income between Lloyd's and OPIC was designed to be comparable to the approach that might be used in setting up a joint underwriting pool. This worked out to give Lloyd's about $2.6 million annual premium income on current-expropriation insurance.[24]

Joint Underwriting

During the summer of 1972, the Insurance Advisory Committee of OPIC's Advisory Council was created to present specific proposals concerning the entry of the private insurance industry into the program. The Advisory Council had previously encouraged OPIC to obtain increased involvement by the private insurance industry in the program, but it was cognizant of the difficulty of formally abandoning access to the U.S. Treasury as long as OPIC was exposed to the risk of catastrophic loss.[25]

The Council's Insurance Advisory Committee made the following recommendations:

    a. The OPIC insurance program cannot and should not be completely transferred to the private sector, in view of the need for long-term coverage commitments, excess loss reinsurance, and assurance that the program's public purposes will be maintained.

    b. The application of the private insurance industry's underwriting expertise to OPIC's operations would be useful.

    c. OPIC should seek private insurance industry participation through creation of an association which would directly write investment insurance, with private members bearing first loss liability up to a stated amount and OPIC bearing excess of loss, or catastrophic liability.

    d. If such an association could be arranged on financial terms satisfactory to both OPIC and the private companies, broad participation by the U.S. insurance industry probably could be achieved in a significant band of expropriation and inconvertibility liabilities but *not* for war risks.

    e. Initially OPIC should handle the association's underwriting and other administrative functions through a management contract.[26]

These recommendations provided the basis for talks between OPIC and the U.S. insurance companies in 1973. However, these talks were impeded by the refusal of the private insurance industry to insure war risks, by an inability to arrive at a mutually acceptable division of premiums, and by disagreement over the legal form and standing of the insurance association. This last problem was particularly thorny since it concerned the applicability of state insurance regulations and laws in addition to the tax liabilities of the association.

Parallel Underwriting

OPIC has also explored an alternative form of joint underwriting. Parallel underwriting involves a standard policy in which the private insurance company insures a specified amount of expropriation and inconvertibility with OPIC covering the rest. If the private insurance company decides not to extend the coverage beyond the initial three-year period, OPIC provides the full coverage for the remaining time period in exchange for an agreed price. OPIC would also provide reinsurance to the private insurers. This method would allow the private insurance industry to have more direct contact with the investing companies than it would in direct combination with OPIC. OPIC argued to Congress that parallel underwriting raised many legal and regulatory issues and would entail a host of cumbersome administrative procedures. Hence, OPIC has not actively pursued this alternative.

Other Privatization Possibilities

OPIC has sought to transfer some of its functions to the private insurance industry in several other ways, the most notable of which are coinsurance and multinationalization. On March 8, 1971, OPIC endorsed a coinsurance program designed to limit the extent of expropriation insurance coverage for large and sensitive projects. The policy reduced coverage from what had been previously available by reducing the term of coverage to twelve years from the original twenty, limiting the coverage to the amount of the original investment (thereby excluding reinvested earnings), and providing for automatic coverage reduction.

A project of over $25 million was considered large. Projects that had received special host country benefits or that were concentrated in certain sectors of the economy, such as utilities, communications, transportation, and mining, were considered sensitive. OPIC asumes that coinsurance encourages the investor to take steps to minimize his risk and undertake loss prevention measures, since the effect of the reduced insurance coverage is to make the investor self-insured in part.

For large, sensitive projects, OPIC adopted a policy providing an alternative type of insurance coverage. The policy provides coverage for expropriation for twenty years on the assumption that these are risks over which the investor has little if any influence. The coverage is for 90 percent of the equity investment during the first three years of the contract. It decreases at the rate of 10 percent a year thereafter until the minimum coverage of 50 percent is reached in the seventh year. The flexibility provided by the general policy is evident in the varying special provisions appearing in insurance contracts made for large or sensitive projects between December 1969 and December 1972. OPIC has also sought to include a first-loss deductible clause in its revised standard contract. The coinsurance in such a contract forces the investor to be self-insured for the first 15 percent of any claim made.

Moreover, OPIC has sought to encourage investors from two or more countries to get together in a joint venture or consortium for an investment project. Such multinational investments, OPIC believes, discourage expropriation because international pressures can be brought to bear on the host country. As a result, OPIC may offer lower insurance rates for large or sensitive projects that are multinational.

The 1974 Act and the Private Insurance Industry

Much of what the 1974 act required with respect to increasing the participation of private insurers in insuring political risk had been suggested by OPIC itself. In response to congressional requirements, OPIC drew up and proposed a plan to insurance company representatives at a meeting in Washington, D.C., on August 21, 1974.[27] As a result of this effort, the Overseas Investment Insurance Group (Group) was established on February 14, 1975. The Group—composed of several insurance companies, other insurers, and OPIC—insured only expropriation and inconvertibility risks. Its goal was to make political risk insurance attractive to a skeptical private insurance industry. During its first year, the private insurer members subscribed to a total of $6.55 million of a $40-million-per-country first-loss pool, with OPIC taking up the balance. By 1977 the Group had twenty-one U.S. and European insurers who participated in a pool with net loss retentions of $40 million per country and $80 million total. The private insurer subscription had risen to $10.2 million of the $40-million-per-country first-loss pool.[28] However, OPIC still bore 75 percent of the risk. The Group wrote direct insurance and reinsured most of OPIC's portfolio; OPIC was a member, served as manager, and insured the Group against excess loss. From the perspective of "privatization," Lloyd's of London was the cornerstone of the Group and, along with several other foreign insurers, accounted for two-thirds of the Group's private participation.

OPIC and the Group entered into several reinsurance agreements, which expired on November 30, 1977. The first agreement provided that the Group reinsure OPIC's existing inconvertibility and expropriation policies, except for investments in Jamaica, the Dominican Republic, and Ethiopia, for the first $40 million loss in any one country and up to $80 million in the aggregate for any one year. In return for this coverage, OPIC was assessed 70 percent of the premiums it received for the reinsured contracts. Under a second agreement, OPIC reinsured the Group's insurance for the excess over a $40 million loss in any one country or $80 million in the aggregate in any one year. The cost of this coverage to the Group was 20 percent of the premiums it received.

The 1974 "privatization" mandate sought to take into account the fundamental unfamiliarity of the private insurance companies with the field of political risk insurance. The Congress attempted to provide the industry with the opportunity to gain the necessary experience and only gradually increase its share of the risk insurance.

The private insurance industry looked upon its participation in OPIC's political risk insurance activities as an experiment. It was willing to experiment with expropriation and inconvertibility coverage, but it also made clear its disinclination to enter the war risk market. OPIC's participation was crucial in order to attract the private insurance industry. However, the insurance industry was aware of its leverage over OPIC, given the 1974 statutory requirement that OPIC phase out the direct writing of political risk insurance.

The effort to involve private participation in OPIC's insurance program has been of marginal success. The "privatization" effort depended very heavily on the capacity and willingness of the private insurance industry to accept a substantial, as opposed to a marginal, level of political risk insurance. The U.S. private insurance industry's basic lack of knowledge of the political risk field and the likelihood that conventional risk principles are inapplicable to political risk insurance contributed heavily to OPIC's inability to comply with the congressional "privatization" mandate. Even within the Group's insurance program, private participation reached only 25 percent after three years. Furthermore, the bulk of private participation came from foreign and not U.S. insurance companies.

With the termination of the 1974 statutory mandate requiring OPIC to transfer its insurance program to the private insurance industry, OPIC has resumed its primary role of first-line insurer but will also continue to cooperate with private insurers through reinsurance agreements. The Overseas Investment Insurance Group was disbanded in November 1977, and the Overseas Investment Reinsurance Group was formed on December 1, 1977. The new reinsurance group includes fourteen U.S. and European private insurance companies. It will reinsure up to $5.3 million of OPIC's expropriation and inconvertiblity losses, subject to liability limits based on their pro rata shares of $10 million per project, $40 million per country, and $80 million globally per year.[29]

The 1977 Congressional Hearings

Unlike the 1973 congressional hearings, the 1977 congressional hearings seemed to indicate a basic consensus concerning OPIC's functions and purposes. Furthermore, while on October 25, 1977, the Senate approved OPIC's extension by a wide margin of 69 to 12, the House treated OPIC with some skepticism and confronted OPIC with considerable opposition, although it too passed its version of the bill by a vote of 191 to 165 on February 23, 1978.

The focus of the 1977-1978 congressional hearings was OPIC's development purposes, not its "privatization" goals. In preparation for these hearings, the Carter administration conducted an interagency review of OPIC. This review concluded that OPIC can advance important U.S. foreign economic policy objectives. However, in order to do so, OPIC, according to the Carter administration, required a different emphasis in three areas:

1. OPIC should focus much more heavily on the poorer developing countries which really need its assistance. However, OPIC's developmental objectives cannot be realized under the "privatization" guidelines,
2. OPIC should develop innovative risk reducing coverage for projects in energy and other raw materials, and
3. Because of the limited participation by private insurance companies, OPIC cannot successfully pursue its objectives and turn over its entire insurance portfolio to the private sector by the end of 1980. Therefore, the new legislation should eliminate the "privatization" objective dictated by the 1974 law.

The House Committee on International Relations held hearings in 1977 on H.R. 9179, which would extend OPIC's authority to conduct its programs through September 30, 1980, and which would also modify the guidelines for these programs.[30] The Senate's Committee on Foreign Relations held hearings on S. 1771.[31]

Even though the House bill extended OPIC for three years and the Senate bill for four years, H.R. 9179 and S. 1771 were in fundamental accord. Each of the bills

1. contained provisions for eliminating the 1974 statutory "privatization" requirement,
2. provided for the restructuring of OPIC's development mandate,
3. stated that payment of any claimant found to be responsible for an act of bribery would be prohibited, and
4. provided for OPIC involvement in mineral extraction projects.[32]

Both the Senate and House subcommittees repeatedly pointed out that OPIC's primary goal should be to facilitate the flow of U.S. capital and skill into LDCs in order to aid the economic and social development of these countries. The Senate subcommittee observed that the U.S. government has had a consistent policy of promoting the flow of private investment to developing

countries. In fact, part of the U.S. overall development assistance
program has been to strengthen the private sector in LDCs,
notwithstanding some criticism that the developmental impact is
not necessarily beneficial.

The House committee strongly supported the Carter administration's view that OPIC should focus much more heavily on the
poorer LDCs, but seemed doubtful that this policy would in fact
be implemented despite OPIC's new guidelines. The House
committee favored restricting OPIC's programs in the richer
LDCs and suggested that OPIC should become involved in those
countries "only in limited cases where the benefits to the country
are overwhelmingly demonstrable and OPIC's presence clearly
will make a difference."[33]

OPIC's representatives did not satisfy the House committee
that OPIC was effectively carrying out its development goal in a
way that complements the development assistance objectives of
the United States. OPIC's small development office was
considered inadequate to evaluate proposed projects from a
development perspective. However, the House committee criti-
cized the Congress as a whole for not providing OPIC with
adequate guidelines. Therefore, H.R. 9179 "contains a provision
requiring OPIC specifically to take account of the development
effects of its actions, setting forth specific development criteria to
guide OPIC decision making, and requiring OPIC to maintain a
Development Impact Profile on each of its projects and to submit
an annual development impact analysis to Congress."[34]

The Senate committee agreed that there is a strong need for an
analysis of the developmental impact of OPIC-supported
projects. In full accord with the House committee, it suggested
that OPIC should improve its analyses in order to be able to select
projects with maximum developmental impact. However, it
believed that the factors listed by the House committee were too
detailed and preferred an approach that stressed more general
social and economic development goals.

The House committee concluded that the private insurance
industry would not take over all of OPIC's insurance programs.
Therefore, it agreed with the Carter administration's request to
repeal the privatization requirements and deadlines. Futher-
more, H.R. 9179 required that OPIC end the joint direct
underwriting arrangements it had made with the private insurers.

The Senate committee stressed that the "privatization" mandate had significantly restricted OPIC's developmental objectives. Because of the requirement to attract private insurers, OPIC's risk management principles attracted it to the less risky projects in the richer LDCs rather than the more risky but more developmental projects in the poorer LDCs. Despite OPIC's failure to obtain a complete "privatization" of its programs, the Senate committee wanted OPIC to continue the "beneficial risk-sharing aspects of privatization."[35] However, the conference report adopted the House provision.

The House committee remained uncertain whether the availability of OPIC insurance coverage makes any difference whether an investment project is undertaken. Its staff studies indicated that OPIC insurance made little, if any, impact, but it had heard testimony indicating that for certain investors, OPIC programs do make a difference.

The House committee argued that OPIC should play a more significant part in the investment decisions of small and medium-sized firms. It expressed its expectations that OPIC give preferential consideration to companies not on the Fortune 1000 list. It also emphasized such other restrictions on OPIC as denying coverage to "runaway plants" or to investment projects that would unfavorably affect the U.S. balance of payments or U.S. employment.

As part of its risk minimization policy, OPIC had limited coverage for "large and sensitive projects." Extractive industries, which are highly susceptible to expropriation and other adverse political actions, make up the bulk of these projects. OPIC wrote less insurance for extractive industries than AID had—which may be due to a combination of the LDCs' participation and ownership requirements as well as OPIC's risk minimization policy. As a result of policies adopted by the Carter administration, Congress, and OPIC in 1977, however, OPIC may increase its insurance coverage for the extractive industry. In 1974 the criticism had focused on OPIC's exposure in the sensitive extractive industry; in 1977 the argument was quite the contrary. In fact, a GAO report, after pointing to U.S. dependence on imports of five critical minerals, argues that by restricting coverage on "large and sensitive projects," OPIC has reduced its high-risk insurance policies but has also simultaneously reduced the potential economic and developmental impact in the LDCs. Furthermore, the loss of the potential supply of raw materials from these LDCs to the United States is a major disadvantage for the United States.

The Senate subcommittee gave its support to encouraging mineral production in the LDCs in order to increase production and to diversify the sources of supply. The House subcommittee also supported the Carter administration's proposal to increase OPIC's involvement in the mining sector in order to counter a misallocation of resources. Because mining operations in such countries as Chile, Zaire, Peru, Zambia, and Venezuela have been major targets of expropriation, private companies have preferred to develop the less productive and more expensive deposits in a few developed countries rather than confront the political risk involved in exploiting richer reserves in LDCs. Consequently, during the 1970s, 80 percent of mining exploration expenditures have been concentrated in such developed countries as the United States, Australia, Canada, and South Africa.

The disagreements between the House and Senate versions over OPIC's activities were resolved in conference and filed on April 5, 1978. The House and Senate agreed on the bill, and the president signed it into law. The key provisions of the Overseas Private Investment Corporation Act of 1978 provide that

> The Corporation, in determining whether to provide insurance, financing, or reinsurance for a project, shall especially—
>
> (1) be guided by the economic and social development impact and benefits of such a project and the ways in which such a project complements, or is compatible with, other development assistance programs or projects of the United States or other donors; and
>
> (2) give preferential consideration to investment projects in less developed countries that have per capita incomes of $520 or less in 1975 United States dollars, and restrict its activities with respect to investment projects in less developed countries that have per capita incomes of $1,000 or more in 1975 United States dollars [Sec. 231].

The bill also calls upon OPIC

> (e) to the maximum degree possible consistent with its purposes—

(1) to give preferential consideration in its investment insurance, reinsurance, and guaranty activities to investment projects sponsored or involving United States small business; and
(2) to increase the proportion of projects sponsored by or significantly involving United States small business to at least 30 percent of all projects insured, reinsured, or guaranteed by the Corporation [Sec. 231].

Other provisions that have become law are that (1) OPIC's direct loan authority is limited to U.S. small businesses or cooperatives, and (2) OPIC is authorized to allocate up to one-half of its annual net income to facilitate developmental projects proposed by small U.S. businesses. In addition, the 1974 statutory privatization mandate has been terminated, and OPIC must prepare and maintain a development impact profile for each investment project. Furthermore, the bribery provision requires OPIC to deny claims under future insurance contracts for losses resulting from an act for which the investor or its agent has been convicted under the 1977 Foreign Corrupt Practices Act. OPIC is also prohibited from supporting any exploration, mining, or other extraction of copper as well as any projects involving palm oil, sugar, or citrus for export to the United States.

Extent of Liability

The major push for privatization was prompted by events in Chile. However, fear concerning OPIC's exposure did not abate as a result of OPIC's agreements with the Group: "Although it is highly unlikely that any great portion of the worldwide total would be subject to claims at one time, it is not improbable that this could occur in any one country, as it did recently in Chile."[36] In fact, expropriations in such countries as Cuba, Egypt, and Chile suggest that massive and sweeping expropriation is associated with radical systemic political change in one country. Notwithstanding the agreements with the Group, OPIC's potential liability from sweeping expropriation in a single country still subjected OPIC to the very catastrophic liability that the "privatization" mandate was supposed to alleviate. In short, OPIC remained the primary insurer for catastrophic losses. With the congressional approval for the abandonment of the original "privatization" mandate, OPIC will still remain exposed to potential catastrophic losses occurring in a single country. If the claims against OPIC exceed OPIC's reserves and if OPIC cannot delay payment for the claims, the U.S. Treasury—that is, the U.S. taxpayer—would be the ultimate reinsurer. OPIC pledges the "full faith and credit" of the U.S. government to meet the obligations when OPIC reserves cannot pay for them. Because of the uncertainties surrounding OPIC's liabilities, the comptroller general of the United States writes that he is "not able to express an opinion on the adequacy of the amount reserved for losses the Corporation may suffer because of its insurance and guaranty contract."[37]

OPIC's supporters claim that it serves an extremely useful function in resolving conflicts between host countries and investors. OPIC's own preference is to allow the investor and the host country to resolve their conflicts when a dispute arises. Where a satisfactory resolution is not achieved, however, OPIC will directly involve itself in the negotiations if requested by the investor. Some argue that if OPIC were not involved in the claims settlement function, investors might seek to involve such U.S. government bodies as the State Department and the home government-host government conflict would perhaps be exacerbated.

OPIC's supporters also emphasize its role in securing raw materials. If OPIC can coordinate with its foreign counterpart agencies, "it can multilateralize the deterrent by getting a number of governments in support of firms from a variety of countries and therefore reduce the risk of nationalization."[38] Furthermore, it may also be able to encourage investors to abandon the 100 percent ownership approach in favor of such alternatives as production sharing, service contracts, and management operations.

OPIC's critics argue that OPIC serves as a government subsidy for MNEs. To the degree that the U.S. government is providing a service that private industry is not willing to provide, the argument may have merit. However, other countries have developed programs similar to OPIC to help their companies compete for markets and access to raw materials. To lessen the encouragement for U.S. investments in the LDCs would make little sense at a time when commercial relations with raw material-supplying countries are becoming increasingly important to the United States. This is one of the major factors that has prompted both the Carter administration and the Congress to support, with qualifications, OPIC's continued existence. If OPIC's operations are severely restricted, it has been argued, U.S. foreign investors will be placed at a competitive disadvantage vis-à-vis their foreign counterparts who have access to their foreign governments' investment insurance programs and subsidies, especially in capital-rich, but technologically poor countries.

Yet the evidence that U.S. access to raw materials is improved by having U.S.-based MNEs exploit these resources overseas is hardly conclusive. During the 1973 oil embargo the United States received no benefit from the fact that U.S.-based MNEs were exploiting the oil. In fact, despite the power attributed to MNEs, even a weak host country can exert considerable control over its resources, especially raw materials.

The entire controversy over OPIC may be out of proportion to the role it actually plays. Even though the U.S. insurance program is larger than those of other countries, it has steadily declined in relation to the total volume of U.S. investments. In 1971, approximately 36 percent of U.S. investments in developing countries carried OPIC insurance. By 1973, however, that figure had fallen to 8 percent, and by 1975 to about 6 percent. Arguably, therefore, government insurance is not essential to the bulk of U.S. firms that invest in developing countries, as MNEs themselves bear more and more of their political risk exposure.[39]

3
Political Risk: Identifying and Defining the Issue

International corporate executives face governmental institutions and a variety of risks that distinguish their task from that of domestic corporate executives. Many view political risk in terms of government interference, through specific acts or events, with the conduct of business or in terms of overall government policy and attitude toward foreign investors. The international corporate executive is likely to view the international and host country environments as adding additional and difficult dimensions to the conduct of business operations. The increasing role of governments in the regulation of business justifies this perception.

Identification and Assessment of "Political Risk"

A general awareness of the political risk problem has stimulated a variety of efforts to understand and deal with its complexity. For some, political risk is best illustrated by "politically caused" losses—for example: "(1) confiscation of property without adequate compensation, (2) damage to property or actions against personnel, (3) governmental interference with the terms of privately negotiated contracts, (4) bans on remittances of currency, and (5) discriminatory taxation or other arbitrary requirements on the firm."[1]

Others, however, may search for the fundamental cause of these losses and point to a factor such as political instability. Having isolated this factor, they may then focus on the familiar trilogy of various social, political, and economic factors as tending to cause instability: "(1) strong internal factions (religious, racial, language, tribal, or economic), (2) social unrest and disorder, (3) recent or impending independence, (4) new international alliances and relations with neighboring countries, (5) forthcoming elections, (6) extreme programmes, (7) vested interests of local business groups, and (8) proximity to armed conflict."[2]

In this chapter we will review many of the recent attempts to cope with the issue of political risk. One of the many problems encountered in trying to analyze political risk is the semantic confusion surrounding the concept itself. We will try to clarify the concept. A clearer understanding of the concept and the phenomena encompassed should substantially promote the ability to analyze the problem. We will first review the "political" dimension and then proceed to the "risk" dimension.

The concept of political risk encompasses more than the risk of expropriation. Nevertheless, the fear of expropriation plays a pervasive and dominant role in shaping the attitudes of many overseas investors.

Bruce Lloyd distinguishes between expropriation and nationalization.[3] He defines expropriation, on the one hand, as a discriminatory action against a particular firm listed in a government decree. Nationalization, on the other hand, is directed against a sector of the economy rather than against a particular firm.

Expropriation is a recognized legal right of any sovereign government; but the taking of private, foreign-owned property must normally be for the public interest, and the private owners must be given "prompt, adequate, and effective compensation." Nevertheless, the specter of expropriation often clouds the political risk issue for corporate managers, especially since it is one of the most radical changes in the "rules of the game." MNEs often find themselves attempting to implement remedial measures once the threat of expropriation is imminent. A long-run policy of good corporate citizenship might well result in a more productive preventive program. However, because of the dramatic danger it poses, expropriation remains the most discussed political risk phenomenon. The overpublicized aspect of expropriation should not be allowed to shift corporate attention from the other less obvious, yet at least equally important, political risk factors.

During the 1960s MNEs as well as the U.S. government became increasingly concerned with the issue of political risk. Their anxiety was heightened by the 1971 events in Chile. Yet before 1975 there were very few relevant academic or corporate efforts to analyze or provide a theoretical explanation for political risk. In 1972 one business professor wrote, "The role of political phenomena in the international operations of U.S. firms has not received extensive inquiry from either academics or practitioners. . . . The literature which attempts to identify actual relationships between political phenomena and international business behavior is practically non-existent."[4]

Most of the literature on political risk has been produced by business professors, published in academically oriented business journals, and geared primarily to other business professors. Even though some businessmen have benefited from some of this literature, the business community as a whole has had little exposure to the "political" aspect of political risk. Furthermore, much of this literature has viewed political risk primarily from the perspective of the MNEs. Although practitioners hired by MNEs are rightly concerned with the MNEs' point of view, political risk can and should also be viewed from the perspective of other key institutions, such as the host country, the U.S. government, and the insurance industry.

Many writers on political risk tend to view it as a particular unwanted event or as the probability of a particular unwanted event. Indeed, some depict political risk as nothing more than a political activity or event that might give rise to risk. A more fruitful approach, we suggest, is to consider political risk as the combined probabilities of an entire set of unwanted events. In addition, political risk should not be viewed as a static occurrence, but rather as a dynamic problem. The likelihood of political *change* as it affects the investment is, in fact, the core of the political analyst's problem-solving goal.

We begin the review of the political risk literature by examining three representative writers on political risk: Franklin Root, Stefan Robock, and Robert Green. Each seeks to identify and define crude categories of political risk, and each gives some analysis of the causes of political risk. But neither individually nor collectively have they provided a systematic analysis of either the concept or its implications. Moreover, the authors seem to have generated considerable confusion about what constitutes a "political risk." Accordingly, each author has a wide variety of proposed corporate responses.

Franklin Root focuses on the sources of the international manager's probability judgments about future political conditions and events in a host country:

> Broadly speaking, political uncertainty for the international manager refers to the *possible* occurrence of political events of any kind (such as war, revolution, coup d'etat, expropriation, taxation, devaluation, exchange control, and import restrictions) at home or abroad that would cause a loss of profit potential and/or assets in international business operations. . . . When the international manager makes a probability judgment of an uncertain political event in a host country, he thereby converts a political uncertainty into a political *risk*.[5]

Root has developed three categories of political uncertainty depending on how they affect the firm: (1) transfer, (2) operational, and (3) ownership/control. Although transfer and operational uncertainties are likely to result from political/economic risks, Root also argues that ownership/control uncertainties are likely to result from political/social risks. He also seeks to describe how management weighs opportunity and risk factors in a given situation. He concludes that the major reason for a company's investment overseas is the retention of a foreign market that could not be adequately maintained solely by direct exports from the United States; in such cases, a company perceives that its investment return opportunity outweighs the business and political risk it will face in that particular country. In addition, Root found that market opportunity and assessment of political risk are the major factors considered in a company's overseas investment decision.

Root also suggests that corporate responses to "political risk" can be divided into three behavioral categories: (1) avoidance, (2) adaptation, and (3) risk transfer. The critical factor explaining the behavior the company will choose in its investment decision is its perception of "political risk." The behavior of company executives in calculating the "political risks" associated with foreign investment causes Root to lament that "no executive offered any evidence of a *systematic* evaluation of political risks, involving their identification, their likely incidence, and their specific consequences for company operations. In a formal sense, at least, American companies do not appear to go much beyond a general recognition of political risks and an ill-defined appraisal of their significance."[6] Although Root has acknowledged the difficulty of separating political and economic risk at the level of implementation, he still maintains that political uncertainty describes either a potential government act or the general instability of the political or social system.[7]

Many companies seek to transfer political risk to other parties. Of the companies with foreign production facilities that Root had studied, however, over half had never insured against the three kinds of political risk—that is, inconvertibility, expropriation, and war—covered by the investment insurance program. Rather than transferring the risks through insurance, the unprotected companies were in fact relying on avoidance or adaptation techniques—such as transfer pricing, quick extraction of profits, and joint ventures—to minimize potential threats to their investments.

The corporate calculation of the benefits associated with risk transfer through investment insurance as opposed to adaptation or avoidance techniques, Root argues, is relatively unaffected by the cost of the insurance: "It is questionable, however, whether lower cost guaranties would cause much shift from avoidance to risk-transfer, because most executives do not view investment guaranties as an incentive or inducement to invest. A management that is not attracted to a developing country by its perception of market opportunity is not going to invest there even if guaranties are cost-free."[8] The accurate identification of "political risks," the manner in which probabilities are assigned to each political risk, and the selection of appropriate corporate responses—Root views all as crucial to the foreign investment decision process.

In his conclusion, Root emphasizes that the lack of systematic study and evaluation of political risk by American management preserves the gap between an investor's perception of political risk and the *real* amount of political risk any particular investment faces. Implicit in this appraisal is Root's belief that sufficient information can be gathered so that political risk can be analyzed through methods similar to those used for economic or business risks.

Stefan Robock has attempted to develop an improved conceptual framework to identify "political risks," forecast their occurrence, and render them a more objective element in decision making.[9] Robock's conceptual framework for the analysis of "political risk" concerns: (1) the sources of political risk, (2) the groups through which political risk can be generated, and (3) the effects of political risk, that is, the types of influence on international business operations. Table 3.1 outlines Robock's conceptual framework. Given his background, Robock is better versed in the effects of political events on business operations than he is on the political and social conditions that give rise to these events. The sources of political risk tend to be of secondary or tertiary importance. Nevertheless, he offers some useful distinctions among types of political risk and some insights into the relationship between political instability and political risk.

Robock draws a significant, although gross, distinction between macro and micro "political risks." Macropolitical risks he defines as unanticipated and politically motivated environmental changes broadly directed at all foreign enterprises. Micropolitical risks are environmental changes intended to affect only selected business fields or foreign enterprises with specific characteristics. An example of the former is the actions Castro took on assuming power; an example of the latter is Chile, where economic nationalism in the late 1960s and early 1970s seemed directed primarily against foreign mining concerns in the country.

Robock contends that political instability, in and of itself, is not a reliable index of political risk, since changes in the national leadership are not necessarily destabilizing for the broader political environment in which investments operate. He distinguishes between political instability and political risk by noting that those political changes that do not significantly alter the business environment do not constitute a risk for international business. For better forecasts of political risk, he argues, different criteria should be chosen for the evaluation of political instability in each political system. He identifies four basic steps in political risk forecasting:

First, an understanding of the type of government presently in

TABLE 3.1

OUTLINE OF ROBOCK'S CONCEPTUAL FRAMEWORK
FOR POLITICAL RISK*

Sources of Political Risk	Groups Through Which Political Risk Can Be Generated	Effects of Political Risk on Business
Competing political philosophies (nationalism, socialism, communism)	Government in power and its operating agencies	Confiscation: loss of assets without compensation
Social unrest and disorder	Parliamentary opposition groups	Expropriation with compensation: loss of freedom to operate
Vested interests of local business groups	Nonparliamentary opposition groups (guerrilla movements)	Operational restrictions (market shares, product characteristics, employment policies, etc.)
Recent and impending political independence	Nonorganized common interest groups (students, workers, peasants, minorities, etc.)	Loss of transfer freedom (financial, goods, personnel or ownership rights)
Armed conflicts and internal rebellions for political power	Foreign governments or intergovernmental agencies such as the EEC	Breaches of or unilateral revisions in contracts and agreements
New international alliances	Foreign governments willing to enter into armed conflict or to support internal rebellion	Discrimination (taxes, compulsory subcontracting, etc.)
		Damage to property or personnel from riots, insurrections, revolutions and wars

*Stefan H. Robock, "Political Risk: Identification and Assessment," Columbia Journal of World Business, July-August 1971; Stefan H. Robock, "Assessing and Forecasting Political Risk," abstract paper for the Research Conference on the Multinational Corporation in the Global Political System, Philadelphia, Pennsylvania, April 22-23, 1971.

power, its patterns of political behavior and its norms for stability;
second, an analysis of the multinational enterprise's own product
or operations to identify the kind of political risk likely to be
involved in particular areas. . . . Third, a determination of the
source of the potential risk. . . . The fourth step is to project into the
future the possibility of political risk in terms of probability and
time horizons.[10]

Robock cites one international company that forecasts political
risk by using two projections. One projection is of the chances
that a particular political group will be in power during specific
forecast periods. The second deals with the type of government
interference that each political group can be expected to generate.
From these estimates, the likely political risk during specific
future periods is calculated. Then the company can adjust the
present value of expected cash flows, or the internal rate of return
from the investment project under consideration, to reflect the
timing and magnitude of the risk probabilities. We deal with
methods for monitoring and integrating political risk analysis in
a cash flow model in Chapter 5.

The international business enterprise, in Robock's view, is not
helpless in confronting political risk. He discusses several
methods by which a company may minimize the effect of
assuming such risks, including:

1. use of investment guaranties,
2. timing and entry strategies,
3. altering the subsidiary's activity,
4. use of international production network strategies,
5. controlling the location of intangible assets,
6. local purchasing strategies,
7. sourcing and movement of funds, and
8. direct lobbying.[11]

Robock's hope is that the intuitive and subjective way in which
international managers often make their overseas investment
decisions can give way to knowledgeable decisions based on a
more comprehensive understanding of political risks and their
effects on particular business activities. He believes that "political
risk" must be treated more objectively if it is to influence the

TABLE 3.2

GREEN'S POLITICAL SYSTEM
CLASSIFICATION SCHEME FOR ESTIMATING
RISK OF RADICAL POLITICAL CHANGE*

I. Modernized Nations
   A. Instrumental-adaptive systems (the United States, United Kingdom)
   B. Instrumental-nonadaptive systems (France, Italy)

II. Modernizing Nations
   A. Instrumental and quasi-instrumental systems attempting adaptive
      politics (India, Turkey, Mexico)
   B. Modernizing autocracies (Spain)
   C. Military dictatorships (Burma, Ghana)
   D. Mobilization systems (China, Cuba)
   E. Recently independent systems (much of Black Africa)

---

*Green's classification nomenclature is drawn from David E. Apter,
The Politics of Modernization, Chicago: University of Chicago Press, 1965,
and Gabriel A. Almond and G. Bingham Powell, Comparative Politics: A
Developmental Approach, Boston: Little, Brown & Co., 1966.

manner in which a corporate decision-maker acts. Although Robock believes that political instability studies by political scientists are of little value to the manager of an international enterprise, Robert Green bases his work on the assumption that the political structure of a society is a crucial factor in determining the political risk to a foreign investment. He asserts that the risk of "radical political change" in a society can be determined from the level of political instability in the given nation.[12] He offers a classification of political systems based on both economic and political characteristics (see Table 3.2), whereby the risk of radical political change increases as one goes down this scale. Green invokes standard economic and political development arguments to support his classification scheme. He does not explicitly draw, however, a relationship between a type of political system and the accompanying degree of political risk to a foreign investor.

Green's prescription for reducing exposure to political risk is to avoid investments in countries on the lower end of his spectrum. Long-term investments in modernizing countries should be made in what he calls quasi-instrumental systems and modernizing autocracies. Short-term, rather than long-term, investments should be considered in military regimes. In fairness to Green, he does not suggest that this method of analysis is valid and comprehensive enough to serve as the primary tool in the assessment of political risk.

Defining "Political Risk"

Root, Robock, and Green offer many insights into political risk, but their works reveal some shortcomings. Each has avoided in some measure the difficult task of defining precisely what is meant by the term *political risk*. For example, Green deals only with a small subset—radical political change—of all the events that contribute to political risk. Robock offers an "operational" definition of political risk, noting that "political risk in international business exists (1) when discontinuities occur in the business environment, (2) when they are difficult to anticipate, and (3) when they result from political change. To constitute a 'risk' these changes in the business environment must have the potential for significantly affecting the profit or other goals of a particular enterprise."[13]

Robock makes a significant contribution by pointing out the dynamic nature of a political environment. However, it is difficult to accept Robock's implicit contention that all unanticipated discontinuities in the business environment that result in political change can be considered "political risks." Even if one chooses to label all unanticipated political change "political risk," it is important to realize that certain types of political change may adversely affect foreign investments and other types may not. In fact, certain types of political change may improve conditions for business enterprises. Furthermore, the same political event may directly benefit one corporation while adversely affecting another. A particular firm's goals, product, and position within the host country, for example, may play a major role in determining the political risk it faces. In short, corporate decision-makers concerned with political events should concern themselves with the question, "How will political events affect *my* firm?"

Although identifying the sources of "political risk," Franklin Root skirts the problem of definition. He notes that a company investing abroad faces "a wide spectrum of political risks that are generated by the attitudes, policies, and overt behavior of host governments and other local power centers such as rival political parties, labor unions, and nationalistic groups."[14]

Greene defines political risk as "that uncertainty stemming from unanticipated and unexpected acts of governments or other organizations which may cause loss to the business firm."[15] This definition of political risk assumes loss to the business enterprise, but, as pointed out earlier, the definition advanced here includes the possibility of loss but also the opportunity for gain.

These varying definitions of the same term obviously suggest that there is considerable ambiguity, if not confusion, over what political risk is. Clearly, the distinction has *not* been made between the *probability* of occurrence of an undesired political event(s) and the *uncertainty* generated by inadequate information concerning the occurrence of such an event(s). Yet this distinction, which some have termed an objective as opposed to a subjective risk estimate, is crucial to political risk assessment.

Knowledge of the political environment in which the business operates or will operate can reduce the uncertainty involved in decisions about overseas investment. Although the processing of the information is unquestionably subjective, this knowledge allows the businessman to make better calculations regarding the probability that certain types of undesirable political events will occur. Moreover, the businessman should also be monitoring political events that would allow his firm to undertake profitable ventures. The isolation and identification of political factors that can adversely or positively affect the foreign investor is a difficult task, which must be followed by the equally difficult task of measuring and aggregating these factors in a manner allowing for forecasting. If the businessman considering an investment overseas wants knowledge of comparative political risk across countries, he encounters the additional methodological problem of standardizing risk estimates across political systems.

The essential purpose of such efforts is to minimize the uncertainty involved in overseas investment decisions by maximizing the accuracy of political risk estimates. This latter task, however, is difficult to do, in part because of the lack of any systematic analysis of political conditions that have given rise to corporate losses in the past. Certainly, few would deny that comparative assessments of whole political systems present serious difficulties. Logically, the assessment of political risk should include an analysis of the stability of the country's political system, both in terms of its absolute value and in comparison with the political systems of other countries where the investment might be made. The investor should be able to determine not only whether to invest in the country but also in what particular region to locate his facility (since certain regions may have political power groups hostile to foreign investment).

Risk, Uncertainty, and the Investor

The risk aspect of "political risk" is surrounded by even more confusion than that which surrounds the political aspect. Before considering the special risks and uncertainties facing the foreign investor, we should attempt to clarify the respective meanings of risk and uncertainty.

Risk and reward have been and are likely to remain major determinants of the behavior of rational men. The desire to take a chance, to conquer the unknown, and to secure a reward has been a major factor in the development of the entrepreneurial system. As social organizations became increasingly complex, more rational risk-bearing practices, such as insurance, emerged during the seventeenth century.

An ongoing debate in the field of insurance during the past seventy-five years has centered on defining and assessing "risk" and "uncertainty." Even though it is unnecessary to trace this debate in any detail, several distinctions are of value in this respect. The most important of these distinctions is between the "subjective" and "objective" aspects of risk and uncertainty.

Chester Williams, Jr., and Richard Heins define risk as "objective doubt concerning the outcome in a given situation," and uncertainty as "subjective doubt concerning the outcomes during a given period."[16] They argue that if they had defined risk as uncertainty concerning the possible outcome, the distinction between risk and uncertainty would have become a distinction between objective and subjective risk. In *Insurance and Economic*

Theory, Irving Pfeffer also seems to use the objective-subjective distinction to differentiate between risk and uncertainty: "Risk is a combination of hazards and is measured by probability; uncertainty is measured by degree of belief. Risk is a state of the world; uncertainty is a state of the mind."[17]

Alan Willett, one of the pioneers in risk analysis, has systematically examined the various issues associated with the concept of risk. He argues that it is possible to think of risk either in relation to probability or in relation to uncertainty. In ordinary usage, the degree of risk is usually associated with the degree of probability of loss. However, Willett argued for the need "to define risk with reference to the degree of uncertainty about the occurrence of a loss, and not with reference to the degree of probability that it will occur. Risk in this sense is the objective correlative of the subjective uncertainty. It is the uncertainty considered as embodied in the course of events in the external world of which the subjective uncertainty is a more or less faithful interpretation."[18] This definition implies that "the method by which the degree of risk may be ascertained depends upon the relative perfection of the knowledge of preceding conditions."[19]

The uncertainty to which Willett refers imposes costs on society, and the removal of uncertainty is a potential source of gain. This is, of course, the basis of insurance, which can be viewed as an institutionalized method of transferring risk, the chance of loss. This transfer of risk removes some of the economic consequences of risk from one party and places them on another. By pooling these transferred risks, an insurance company is better able to bear any possible loss, since the "uncertainty" as to the occurrence of any one hazard is reduced by the aggregation of a large number of risks. Transferring risk, however, merely shifts some of the consequences of the risk to others and, in general, does nothing to prevent, reduce, or eliminate the risk. For example, the purchaser of life insurance faces the same risk of death but reduces the economic consequences of his death.

Willett points out that

> the effects of the occurrence of disaster is in itself the same, whether
> it was foreseen or not. It is the destruction of a certain amount of
> capital. But the net result of the occurrence of a certain amount of

loss which was definitely foreseen, is different from the net result of
the occurrence of the same amount of loss, plus previous
uncertainty whether it would be greater or smaller. . . . The greater
the probable variation of the actual loss from the average, the
greater the degree of uncertainty.[20]

In Willett's conception of risk and uncertainty, uncertainty is
thus an unwelcome factor in economic enterprises. The
businessman seeks to eliminate uncertainty if possible and to
reduce or transfer it if not. The psychological weight of
uncertainty can logically be displaced by the acquisition of
all available information affecting business conditions. The
net effect of reducing uncertainty is to reduce the effect
of risk as well.

Anyone considering a foreign investment should separate risk
(the probability that a loss will occur) from uncertainty (the
subjective doubt regarding the occurrence of such a loss). At least
potentially, risk is measurable, insurable, and avoidable;
uncertainty is not. Yet information bridges the two; the same
information that is useful in accurately calculating risk also
serves to reduce uncertainty. It is crucial, therefore, that the
investor always search for the most complete information
available.

Political Risk and Political Uncertainty

The business community's need to reduce the risks of economic
enterprise has fostered the development of sophisticated skills and
a wide variety of economic and financial tools for information
gathering and processing. Demand analysis, production analysis,
distribution analysis, financial analysis, market segmentation
selection, and market promotion techniques were all pushed to
their present state of development by the desire to reduce
economic and financial risk and to forecast future contingencies
more accurately.

The ideal by which business managers determine whether to
make an investment is generally viewed as quite rational.
Accordingly, it involves such concepts as desired rates of return,
discounted cash flows, and comparison with alternative uses of
funds. It also calculates the factors—such as the probable growth

of the economy and changes in market share—that will bear on the likelihood of the investment's being profitable. In other words, the investor often knows a great deal about the business *risk* he will face, and his relative *uncertainty* is low.

But not all business risk is economic or financial, and other techniques and methods have evolved for dealing with risks that stem from societal or political sources. Labor-management relations have become a prominent field. Public relations techniques and company-community relations have become serious concerns. Techniques for dealing with political elites range from such time-honored ones as bribery and controlling political offices to lobbying and forming industry pressure groups. In general, the aim of the entrepreneur is to structure, or at least to neutralize, the social and political systems in such a way as to improve his operations.

Although basically similar economic and financial techniques for risk reduction can be employed in different countries and societies, techniques to reduce political risk tend to be unique for each society. Obviously, labor-management techniques as applied in a developed state may be totally inappropriate not only in an underdeveloped state but even in another developed state. This also holds true for techniques designed to reduce risks stemming from political sources.

The American entrepreneur operating within U.S. borders can usually concentrate on risk reduction through economic and financial techniques. Reasonable attention to labor-management relations, public relations, and community relations usually precludes any serious risk arising from societal sources. Nevertheless, the competition for comparative advantage among business concerns may continue in the U.S. political arena. With the country's constitutional and legal system basically unchanged, American businessmen are relatively insulated from abrupt and unpredictable risk stemming from political sources, and they have traditionally been more concerned with risk than uncertainty. Furthermore, they worry about risk stemming from economic and financial sources rather than risk arising from societal and political origins.

There was a time when an American MNE did not feel it had to bother with political risk in its overseas operations. Whether this feeling resulted from the protection afforded by U.S. gunboat diplomacy or from operating in blissful ignorance of the consequences of political risk, today's U.S.-based MNEs realize that they can no longer afford the luxury of ignoring the political risk posed by both the *host* and *home* countries. In the past they could generate a high rate of return on overseas investments without taking political conditions into account, but now many MNEs, partly through bitter experience, know the importance of evaluating and assessing political risk. However, today's MNEs must be careful not to succumb to the temptation of withdrawing from foreign investments—and thereby of passing up profitable opportunities—because of the specter of political risk. An MNE that fails to consider political events systematically may overlook attractive and profitable overseas investment opportunities because of some irrational fear; or it may proceed with an investment in an area where political events will cause it severe losses.

Ordinarily, as has been noted, the businessman should seek all relevant information about business conditions, estimate both the political and the economic risk, and then decide whether to bear it, attempt to transfer a portion of it, or seek to avoid bearing it altogether. High uncertainty, however, complicates this process. Estimating risk is difficult, making decisions on what portion of risk to bear is arduous, and the temptation to transfer as much of the risk as possible is high. The fact that in the corporate world many investment decisions are made because of the impressions, biases, or whims of senior management does not detract from the value of the ideal or rational investment model.[21] This observation assumes, of course, that investment decisions based on systematic evaluations will yield better results than those made by sheer chance.

The Effects of Risk and Uncertainty on Investment

The effects of risk and uncertainty on investment decisions can perhaps best be illustrated by one concrete example and one hypothetical example. The heavy U.S. investment in Puerto Rico in the last two decades can be attributed in large part to investors' calculations of low risk and perceptions of low uncertainty. Puerto Rico is U.S. territory, it enjoys constitutional protection, and it adheres to familiar legal processes. Most investors see no risk of arbitrary confiscations or expropriations and comparatively little risk of political turmoil. They feel relatively free of all those fears and uncertainties that are often generated by an unfamiliar environment, despite the recent demands for Puerto Rico's independence. Puerto Rico is thus an appealing haven, especially for smaller corporations that do not have the experience of larger firms in dealing with political risk and that often have proportionately more to lose if they miscalculate.

When an American investor ventures abroad into a Third World country, he faces a far different situation. Accustomed to the rule of law, he often encounters the arbitrary and capricious rule of men. Furthermore, today's ruler may not be tomorow's ruler. Uncertainty about the occurrence of loss often concerns him far more than the probability that a loss will occur. Partly because of differences in culture, language, laws, customs, and mores, he knows far less about the social and political environment in which his investment will be made than about the environment in the United States or Puerto Rico. Because of his difficulty in selecting, processing, and analyzing relevant political information, he feels even more uncertain. In short, his bewilderment may prevent him from considering certain countries as possible investment choices.

One fruitful way of examining how political risks and uncertainties are involved in an investment decision is to view that process as a series of steps. A corporation may decide that the best way to increase earnings is to invest internally in order to increase capacity and thereby capture a greater market share. Based on a variety of projections—for example, the situation of the market, the growth of the economy, cost increases in raw materials, and transportation costs—it decides to invest abroad in an LDC. Once again, it must make economic and business calculations and estimate the rate of return. Although it could ignore or implicitly consider the level of political risk of a U.S. investment, it should more explicitly estimate this risk for an overseas investment, for an LDC in particular. For example, it may calculate the rate of return over the life of the investment, but it may be uncertain as to the survival of the investment. Events such as expropriation, nationalization, or increased taxation might substantially reduce the productive life of its investment abroad. Though recognizing the importance of political factors, the corporation for the most part fails to incorporate them systematically—as it does other risks—in its calculation of the profitability of an investment. It can deal with such factors in several ways: (1) ignore the political factors, (2) guess at the likely occurrence of certain disruptive political events, or (3) try to estimate and measure the political risk in some systematic fashion.

Today few corporations considering an investment abroad will totally ignore political factors. At the very least, they will take a guess. They may call in a political consultant, check an investment guidebook, or visit the appropriate State Department desk. Generally, their efforts yield little more than aggregated, random guesses, guesses that not only fail to produce probability estimates of political risk but that may, in fact, have the unfortunate side effect of increasing the uncertainty. When compared with economic risk assessments, such guesses are, at best, imprecise. To a considerable extent, the uncertainty surrounding these political "guesstimates" confounds the calculations of economic risk and economic rewards. The projected return of a corporations's proposed investment is thereby likely to be tainted.

Before considering how a corporation should deal with political factors, it is useful to draw on a distinction made by two utility theorists concerning ideal risk and uncertainty conditions. In *Games and Decisions*, Luce and Raiffa note that the decision-maker is in the *realm of risk* if each course of action leads to one of a set of possible specific outcomes, with each outcome occurring with a known probability.[22] A decision-maker is in the *realm of uncertainty* if each course of action has as its consequence a set of possible specific outcomes, but the probabilities of these outcomes are completely unknown or are not meaningful. In other words, if enough objective information is available to calculate probabilities, one is in the realm of risk. If there is not enough, or if the information is purely subjective, however, one is in the realm of uncertainty. By reducing uncertainties in the political environment to probability terms, political risk analysis provides a mechanism for the objective evaluation of foreign investment climates.

A corporation can attempt to deal with political risk in a systematic fashion by developing an explicit measure of risk based on criteria that are as objective as possible. It should also make the additional effort to tailor the various risk criteria to those factors that are likely to affect its profitability. In short, it should try to move from the realm of uncertainty toward the realm of risk. The measurement of political risk should be an integral part of the assessment of overall investment risk. Although the occurrence of political phenomena cannot be reduced to actuarial tables, political trends can be mapped, and theoretically reasonable, quantifiable forecasts can be made. Further efforts can be made to fit different scenarios and forecasts into computer simulations of prospective investments. For example, political risk analysts may be able to employ methods by which potential host countries can be ranked in terms of the probability that invested funds will be lost through war, expropriation, or nationalization. This ranking can be based on past experiences or on current indicators that point to stress or instability in a political system. To reflect subjective elements better, the political risk analyst might design a "confidence estimate," a subjective measure of the accuracy of the computed probability. This estimate could reflect the "uncertainty" associated with a political risk assessment and could be considered along with the "risk" aspects to provide an even more accurate evaluation of political risk.

Assessing political risk is only part of the picture. The other, if not more important, part is whether and how the enterprise evaluates and uses the assessment. A corporation should have the organizational capacity to generate and properly evaluate political risk estimates. It can create this capacity by forming an investment evaluation team that has an appreciation and broad-based understanding of the political world and the tools of political analysis. This team can be an ad hoc unit established and dismantled for each investment decision, or it can be a permanent unit within the corporate planning staff. In either case, it would use an explicit measurement approach to the assessment of political risk and would seek to integrate the political risk measure into the corporation's modified calculation of rates of return. Even though a systematic analysis of political risk may be reduced to a probability figure, the overall assessment is likely to demand both *qualitative* and *quantitative* treatment of all the essential, available information. If necessary, these rates of return could be evaluated and compared across several countries, with a probability attached to each of the projected return rates. Selecting the appropriate host country for the proposed investment then would become less difficult, as trade-offs between investing in countries with higher economic risks and lower political risks, or vice versa, would become evident.

Political risk should not dominate the investment decision process. MNEs invest overseas for many reasons. However, even though such primary investment considerations as marketing and finance merit the most careful analysis, the argument here is simply that political factors must be systematically analyzed in order to determine, at the very least, whether political factors will interfere with the projected profitability. Certain corporations, such as those in the extractive industry, do not have the entire spectrum of nation-states as investment choices. They must operate in those countries where the raw materials exist; for them, the choice may be different from a manufacturing corporation that has more countries in which it can consider investing. Even though an extractive corporation has fewer countries it needs to evaluate, it may still find a comparative examination of countries useful in order to analyze a possible trade-off between the richness of the ore available and the political risk it faces. The manufacturing corporation, however, may be especially concerned about labor cost, which will also narrow the number of countries it will consider. In that case, it may examine the trade-off between labor cost and political risk. In any event, this process allows a corporation to make a more rational choice among its investment alternatives.

4
Recent Efforts To Analyze and Measure Political Risk

Since overseas investors are and should be concerned with changes that occur in the investment environment, they must face the issue of how to analyze and measure the problem. In the recent past, project analyses were, for the most part, limited to conventional financial, technical, and economic analyses of the foreign venture. However, as host governments have initiated more frequent and dramatic changes, the MNE has, in turn, become more concerned with the political risk component of the overseas investment risk assessment. As the following example illustrates, the lack of a systematic analysis of political events can lead to unnecessary behavior by MNEs.

Before the Cuban confiscation of U.S.-owned assets in 1959, new U.S. investment flows to Latin America were approximately $338 million. In 1960, largely in reaction to Castro's seizures, this figure dropped to $95 million. In 1962, the net flows were negative, that is, American investors withdrew $32 million. Some of this change may be due to different accounting procedures and investment strategies; nevertheless, investor perception of a more hostile political climate was undoubtedly the major factor in reducing dollar flows. This perception proved to be unjustified, because political risk to foreign investment in most Latin American countries changed very little between 1959 and 1962. But the reaction of U.S. investors to the fear of political risk during those three years damaged both foreign and domestic business interests in Latin America, compromised the effectiveness of public aid flows under the Alliance for Progress, and set back developmental programs throughout the hemisphere.

A more sophisticated evaluation of political risk might have prevented such behavior. Unfortunately, this case is but one of many instances where perceptions of political risk resulting from a particular event have led investors into serious miscalculations. During the past few years, many business executives have begun to realize the value of developing more sophisticated techniques of political risk assessment. A few techniques have been developed and systematically used. Political scientists such as Russett, Banks and Textor, and the Feierabends have developed various quantitative techniques, but these methods have serious limitations in a business context.[1] That is, they focus on the general problem of political instability, which, many analysts and businessmen simply assume, is the most significant form of political risk. However, they do not specifically link political instability to adverse effects in the business environment. Therefore, the international business executive must carefully adjust both the techniques and the results to satisfy his own particular needs.[2] However, the effort is still feeble in light of the value more accurate assessment of political risk has to MNEs, developing countries, insurance companies, banks, OPIC, and the U.S. government.

More accurate measures of political risk could also benefit developing countries. Many MNEs still view investment flows as essentially a product of expected returns to capital discounted for political, economic, and other risks. Accordingly, if a more accurate assessment of political risk were available, capital flows could be smoothed out and discount rates possibly reduced to reflect only financial risk. Consequently, the LDCs could pursue national economic planning and long-term development programs more confidently in an environment in which more foreign corporate capital could be expected to respond to the internal investment environment. Second, more accurate measures of political risk would reveal to an LDC its comparative attractiveness to investors. Its officials could then use this knowledge in designing their investment incentive programs or in rejecting unreasonable investor requests for certain concessions.

More accurate measures of political risk would offer many advantages to corporate investors as well. In many cases, foreign investors underestimate or ignore political risk. Indeed, host governments often seek to obsure the real political risk investors face.[3] In other cases, foreign investors overemphasize political risk. Improved assessments could allow the discount rate to reflect only financial risk, thereby improving the attractiveness of a proposed investment and enlarging the number of productive investment opportunities. Better estimates could also enable the potential investor to compare systematically the levels of risk in different countries that meet the corporation's other criteria before deciding where to locate the investment.

More accurate measurement of political risk might also improve management's ability to respond to risk-increasing political events. A study of management reactions to expropriation threats revealed that few managers felt they could have done anything to prevent expropriation.[4] But accurate forecasts of political risk-associated events could provide managers with an "early warning" of what is to come.

Many techniques used by MNEs to evaluate political risk are crude at best, although several MNEs have made significant improvements recently. Robert Stobaugh has pointed out that a number of U.S.-based MNEs have developed scales to rate countries on the basis of their investment climates.[5] These scales are designed to help the corporate decision-maker decide whether a "premium"—that is, a higher rate of return on investment— should be expected if an investment is to be made. Stobaugh notes that these scales are based solely on the subjective opinions of planning managers in corporate international divisions, not data-based scales of the political risk the company may face.

Accurate measurement and forecasting of political risk should also be very useful to insurance companies considering the potential profitability of the political risk insurance business, and it may help them establish a more realistic basis for premiums. Companies currently writing political kidnapping and ransom insurance, such as Investment Insurance International Ltd., which is a subsidiary of Lloyd's of London, charge premiums that on the average range between 2 and 3 percent of the total coverage granted. Since policies now average approximately $1 million per person and sometimes reach almost $5 million, the premiums are substantial for both the purchasers and the sellers.[6] Yet Lloyd's currently relies on an intuitively derived rate structure that is periodically adjusted.

More accurate measurement of political risk could also aid the

U.S. government and OPIC. OPIC's negotiation posture with private insurance companies could be enhanced if non-OPIC-based assessments of political risk were available. Informed by political risk evaluations, U.S. foreign aid policies intended to encourage investment could be designed more effectively.

In short, nearly all parties concerned with foreign investment stand to gain from accurate measures and forecasts of political risk. Of course, the ideal would be to devise a composite political risk number that could be included wherever such a measure would be useful. However, the varying perspectives and interests of the potential parties make it impossible to construct a single composite political risk index.

The uniqueness of international banking activities indicates the degree to which political risk must be tailored to a corporation's particular needs. Banks extending credit to a foreign country deal with the question of how much exposure to have in any given country and what proportion that exposure should be to the overall global exposure.[7]

The credit exposure is made within country guidelines, guidelines based on factors indicating a country's growth potential as well as economic and political stability. Based on these indicators, the countries are rank-ordered. Many banks use this or a similar type of ranking method as a basis for setting country limits on their exposure. By making credit exposure decisions based on country rankings, many banks have in essence diversified their "investments," thereby establishing a portfolio effect. However, multinational banks may be unique in their ability to operate in so many countries and as a result have the capacity to diversify their portfolio as a means of reducing their risk.

Large multinational banks are in a particularly advantageous position in dealing with political risk. They are in contact with both governments and corporations and are likely to have many sources of information. Their various activities generally provide them with more options than other types of multinational corporations are likely to have.

The large number of countries in which a multinational bank operates allows it to obtain a strong intelligence network for social, financial, economic, and political information. The key, however, is the development of an internal organizational capacity for maintaining and retrieving the information required.

An extremely economical method for acquiring such information is to tap the corporation's own resources. The personnel employed by the international corporation can often provide senior management at corporate headquarters with a wealth of information on political and other factors that may affect the overseas investment or operation. Even though the acquisition of this information may well be a sensitive matter, it can provide substantial help to corporate decision-makers. A simple questionnaire developed to address senior management's concerns and administered on a regular basis is well worth the small cost to the MNE. Although the results of this effort should not be the sole basis for making decisions, they can be readily compared to assessments provided by various services. A small staff within a corporate planning group can use this type of data to advise senior management on international problems and opportunities as well as to devise investment and operational strategies.

An *Argus Capital Market Report* purports to provide a framework for appraising country risk for the purpose of establishing foreign exposure guidelines or making "go/no go" investment decisions.[8] In the *Argus* analysis, country risk is divided into "sovereign risk" and "cross-currency risk," the former being primarily political and the latter primarily economic or financial.

However, the *Argus* study does not, in fact, provide a framework for analysis. Rather, it offers a laundry list of economic indicators, for which data are available, for country risk analysis. These indicators are (1) monetary base, (2) domestic base, (3) foreign reserves, (4) purchasing power parity index, (5) currency-to-deposit ratio, (6) consumer prices as a percent change, (7) balance of payments: goods and services as a percent of GNP, (8) balance of payments: goods and services as a percent of foreign reserves, (9) percent change exports/percent change imports, (10) exports as a percent of GNP, (11) imports as a percent of GNP, (12) foreign factor income payments as a percent of GNP, (13) average tax ratio, (14) government deficit as a percent of GNP, (15) government expenditures, (16) real GNP as a percent change, and

(17) real per capita GNP as a percent change.

Even if these factors arguably "educate the decision-maker and force him to think in terms of the relevant economic fundamentals,"[9] they certainly do not provide a framework for political risk or country risk analysis. This laundry list approach lacks a weighting scheme for the factors. Accordingly, it fails to provide for the relative importance of the factors or a frame of reference for the relationship among them. At best, such ratios may provide indications of improvement or deterioration from a particular benchmark of a country's economic condition.

Approaches to Analyzing and Measuring Political Risk

The challenge of measuring political risk is as substantial as defining it. The measurement of political risk largely depends on its definition. Yet, the definition of what contributes to political risk depends not only on the perspective of the definer but also on a host of other considerations. Since various factors make generalization so difficult, one major approach to the definition and measurement of political risk stresses the unique aspects of a particular investment.

We earlier defined political risk as the risk or probability of occurrence of some political event that will change the profitability of a given investment. A decision tree approach, such as that of Stobaugh, can be used to specify a corporate decision-maker's alternatives as well as his probability estimates regarding the occurrence of various events. The decision tree shown in Figure 4.1 outlines the various possibilities in the relationship between a change in government and confiscation of a firm's property. The probable dollar loss can be calculated by multiplying the expected cash flows for each outcome by the probability of that outcome and determining the present value of this cash flow. After such a determination, a decision-maker can consider with greater confidence options such as making a new investment, liquidating an investment, or taking steps to cut back the firm's exposure.

Although a decision tree approach such as the one presented by Stobaugh is helpful to corporate managers, it is important to note that in the example cited an assumption was made concerning the

Figure 4.1

PROBABILITY ANALYSIS—YEAR ONE: GOVERNMENT OVERTHROW

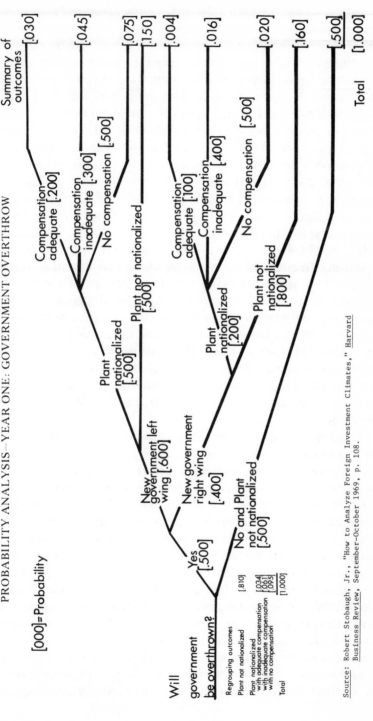

[000]=Probability

Summary of outcomes

Will government be overthrown?

| Compensation adequate [.200] | [.030] |

Plant nationalized [.500]

Compensation inadequate [.300] → [.045]

No compensation [.500] → [.075]

New government left wing [.600]

Plant not nationalized [.500] → [.150]

Yes [.500]

New government right wing [.400]

Compensation adequate [.100] → [.004]

Plant nationalized [.200]

Compensation inadequate [.400] → [.016]

No compensation [.500] → [.020]

Plant not nationalized [.800] → [.160]

No and Plant not nationalized [.500] → [.500]

Total [1.000]

Regrouping outcomes

Plant not nationalized [.810]

Plant nationalized
with adequate compensation [.034]
with inadequate compensation [.061]
with no compensation [.095]

Total [1.000]

Source: Robert Stobaugh, Jr., "How to Analyze Foreign Investment Climates," Harvard Business Review, September–October 1969, p. 108.

factors that would affect the investment. Corporate investors are accustomed to dealing in risk/return types of analyses. They should not be surprised that a systematic approach to political risk analysis calls for an analysis of the factors affecting the investment, their relationship, and the results they yield.

Obviously, the precise set of possible political events affecting a particular investor will be governed, among other factors, by the corporation's definition of the nature and profitability of the investment. Such definitions vary.[10] Some calculate profitability according to repatriated profits; others may view profits in terms of market share within the host country. Thus, some investors may be interested in political events that may affect repatriation of profits; others will be more interested in events that affect internal operations. In either case, the nature of the investment is likely to be important in determining which events are of interest. For example, investments whose productivity depends on factor import or product export will be sensitive to potential changes in trade restrictions. Investments that use factors available in the host country and serve mainly the local markets will be sensitive to changes resulting from shifting political priorities of local elites and to changes resulting from internal political instability (e.g., riots), changes that can threaten the very existence of the enterprise.

Thus, the political events that constitute political risk for a given investor can be uncovered only by a large-scale empirical investigation. A major research effort would be required to assemble an exhaustive list of the independent and dependent variables associated with undesirable political events for a corporation within any given country or group of countries. The difficulty of such an effort has deterred this type of political risk analysis. What little research is done by corporations in particular countries tends to be repetitive. Therefore, very little comprehensive, cumulative knowledge of political risk has been acquired.

Although there will always be a need and market for particularistic studies of political risk, there are also many common risk factors across all types of investment that are of concern to the political risk analyst. This fact has given rise to a second broad, amorphous, intuitive, and somewhat abstract approach to evaluating foreign investment risks. Rather than deal with the complexity of political risk and individual country or investor idiosyncrasies, this approach attempts to provide an overall assessment of the many risks, including political risk, that a foreign investor faces. The two most widely known examples of this approach are the Business Environmental Risk Index (BERI) and the Business International Index of Environmental Risk (BI). Both indexes are based on the "Delphi method" of polling experts for their estimates of environmental risks and then aggregating and weighing their responses. Table 4.1 presents a similar type of rating scale developed by Blasch and Cummings.

The aim of these indexes to present an overall assessment of environmental risks faced by the foreign investor has resulted in reliance on general categories that are of little use in identifying the sources of political risk in any given set of countries or a particular industry. BERI and BI may help investors by presenting broad-brush assessments of economic risks,[11] but their assessment of political risks is less helpful. The BERI index, for example, is composed of fifteen variables grouped into three environmental risk subindexes: political, operations, and financial.

The purpose of the BERI political subindex is to "isolate to the degree possible the political processes affecting business."[12] The six variables composing this subindex are bureaucratic delays, balance of payments, monetary inflation, nationalization, attitudes toward the foreign investor, and profits and political stability. It is notable that three variables—bureaucratic delays, balance-of-payments problems, and monetary inflation—are also components of the financial subindex. Therefore, it is rather doubtful that "double counting" these variables helps the investor isolate the political processes affecting business. Furthermore, the weights given to each of the factors are not justified and seem highly arbitrary. For example, why does the BERI index consider political stability twice as important as nationalization?

The BERI and BI indexes are somewhat better than intuitive and unsystematic judgments of investors who fail to consider political factors altogether. These indexes and various checklists are of some assistance in the identification of factors that may be of importance and are suggestive of how such material may be

TABLE 4.1

CORPORATE RATING SCALE FOR DETERMINING A COUNTRY'S INVESTMENT CLIMATE*

Item	Number of Points Individual Subcategory	Range of Category	Item	Number of Points Individual Subcategory	Range of Category
Capital repatriation:			**Political stability:**		
No restrictions	12	0-12	Stable, long term	12	0-12
Restrictions based only on time	8		Stable, but dependent on		
Restrictions on capital	6		key person	10	
Restrictions on capital and income	4		Internal factions, but		
Heavy restrictions	2		government in control	8	
No repatriation possible	0		Strong external and/or internal		
			pressures that affect policies	4	
Foreign ownership allowed:			Possibility of coup (external and		
			internal) or other radical change	2	
100% allowed and welcomed	12	0-12			
100% allowed, not welcomed	10		**Willingness to grant tariff**		
Majority allowed	8		**protection:**		
50% maximum	6				
Minority only	4		Extensive protection granted	8	2-8
Less than 30%	2		Considerable protection granted,		
No foreign ownership allowed	0		especially to new major industries	6	
			Some protection granted,		
Discrimination and controls,			mainly to new industries	4	
foreign versus domestic business			Little or no protection granted	2	
Foreign treated same as local	12	0-12	**Availability of local capital:**		
Minor restrictions on foreigners,					
no controls	10		Developed capital market; open		
No restrictions on foreigners,			stock exchange	10	0-10
some controls	8		Some local capital available;		
Restrictions and controls on foreigners	6		speculative stock market	8	
Some restrictions and heavy controls			Limited capital market; some		
on foreigners	4		outside funds (IBRD, AID) available	6	
Severe restrictions and controls on			Capital scarce, short term	4	
foreigners	2		Rigid controls over capital	2	
Foreigners not allowed to invest	0		Active capital flight unchecked	0	
Currency stability			**Annual inflation for last**		
			five years:		
Freely convertible	20	4-20			
Less than 10% open/black market			Less than 1%	14	2-14
differential	18		1%-3%	12	
10% to 40% open/black market			3%-7%	10	
differential	14		7%-10%	8	
40% to 100% open/black market			10%-15%	6	
differential	8		15%-35%	4	
Over 100% open/black market			Over 35%	2	
differential	4		Total		8-100

*From Howard Blasch and Joseph Cummings, International Investments: A Research Report, Columbus, Ohio: Society of Insurance Research, 1974.

organized.[13] However, serious methodological problems appear to plague both the BERI and BI indexes. Weighting and scoring procedures are imprecise and highly arbitrary. In dealing with "political stability," for example, each index seems to depend more on the intuitive judgments of the analyst than on any precise specification of what stability is. The BI index asks its panelists to score the political stability of a country along the following scale:

Political Stability

	Score	Weight
a. Long-term stability guaranteed	( )	15
b. Strong government but vulnerable constitution	( )	10
c. Active internal factions	( )	5
d. Strong probability of overthrow (internal and external)	( )	2

The BERI index requires its experts to rate countries' political stability on a five-point scale ranging from 0 (unacceptable conditions) to 4 (superior conditions).

The potential for tremendous variation among the experts in the interpretation of the term *political stability* makes it difficult to interpret the meaning of their scoring. In the BI index, what, for example, does *active internal factions* mean for political stability, and why does it carry only half the weight of *strong government but vulnerable constitution?* Why are certain factors considered and others excluded? What underlying logic supports the four very different categories? In the BERI index, what are *superior conditions?* For whom are they to be judged superior? As such questions indicate, serious problems are associated with these two indexes.

Both the BI and BERI indexes stress a description of existing conditions in the host country and are strongly oriented toward short-term projections of less than a year. This may be of some use to an investor *already* in an LDC, but it is of marginal value to an investor contemplating a longer-term investment. For these, long-term evaluations are essential, and neither the BERI nor the BI index attempts to provide them.

Finally, these two indexes are not very useful in identifying changes in the degree of estimated environmental risk. A correlation of the 1974 BERI and 1972 BI indexes showed a strong relationship to each other.[14] Their ability to differentiate change over time in the risk investors face is thus very limited. Therefore, each of these approaches to the measurement of political risk has inherent limitations for assessing the complexity of political reality in Third World countries.

A viable alternative to these strategies is the measurement of discrete components of political risk that are part of a model. Harald Knudsen has tried to use a components approach. He claims that his "national propensity to expropriate model" integrates political theory and international business theory. He criticizes the "environmental risk approach" of Business International and Business Environmental Risk Index for estimating political risk on the basis of a business climate examined at the time of the investment decision. Knudsen argues that his model presents a means of predicting the future investment climate in advance by examining the country's basic environmental variables as a basis for future political behavior.

He claims that the level of "frustration" is expected to be a function of the difference between level of aspirations and level of welfare and expectations. The "frustration" factor and "scapegoat function of foreign investments" factor are the two factors that explain the national propensity to expropriate, according to this theory, which is depicted in Figure 4.2.[15]

The components approach assumes that political risk, though a product of a very complex set of causal factors, can be broken down into measurable components. Once identified and measured, the components can then be reaggregated in a form suitable to meet the particular needs of the political risk analyst. This components approach is more flexible than either a particular or general approach. It allows the political risk analyst to select those components that are of particular importance to him for a given country or set of countries, yet at the same time it forces the analyst to organize his information in a systematic and aggregated fashion.

The promise and versatility of the components approach can perhaps best be illustrated through a hypothetical example, as in

Figure 4.2

THE NATIONAL PROPENSITY TO EXPROPRIATE MODEL

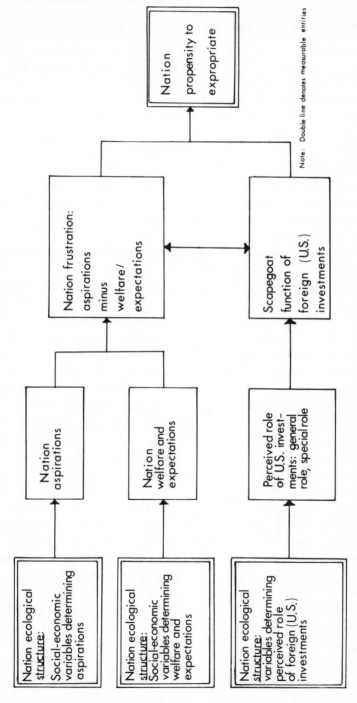

Note: Double line denotes measurable entities

Source: Harald Knudsen, "Explaining the National Propensity to Expropriate: An Ecological Approach," Journal of International Business Studies, Spring 1974.

Figure 4.3.[16] A corporation considers a foreign investment out of a desire to attain one or more goals. It typically requests an evaluation of the potential economic and political risks of a proposed investment. As noted previously, corporate evaluations of economic risks and rewards have reached a high level of sophistication and development. Moreover, the same analytical tools employed to evaluate economic and financial conditions in the United States can be modified and extended to the analysis of these factors in Third World countries. By comparison, the analytical tools needed to estimate social and political risk are less developed, although they have improved recently. Intuition, however, may be an extremely hazardous guide to comparative political analysis.

Complex economic and financial problems of risk estimates are usually broken down into more manageable components to which different techniques of analysis, such as market analysis and modeling, can be applied. The corporate decision-maker can then use the results of such selected analyses to form complex probability estimates of expected return. But social and political risk is rarely broken down into more manageable components to which different techniques of analysis—such as elite analysis, value analysis, and political system stability assessment—can be applied. This is due to many factors, not the least of which is the general unfamiliarity of corporate executives with many social sciences techniques. Ideally, the corporate decision-maker should use the results of political risk analyses to form a composite estimate of the probability of loss or gain due to political factors, just as he does with economic and financial factors.

Once the corporate manager gets the relevant evaluations of economic and political risks, he can examine the trade-off relationships between the estimated risks and rewards of a proposed investment. Based on this consideration and on corporate goals, he can make an informed decision on whether to invest.

On the one hand, if the corporation has tentatively selected a host country, economic and political evaluations of the estimated risks and rewards can analyze local economic and political problems. On the other hand, the corporation may wish to use economic and political risk evaluation techniques to scan a

Figure 4.3

FOREIGN INVESTMENT DECISION FLOW

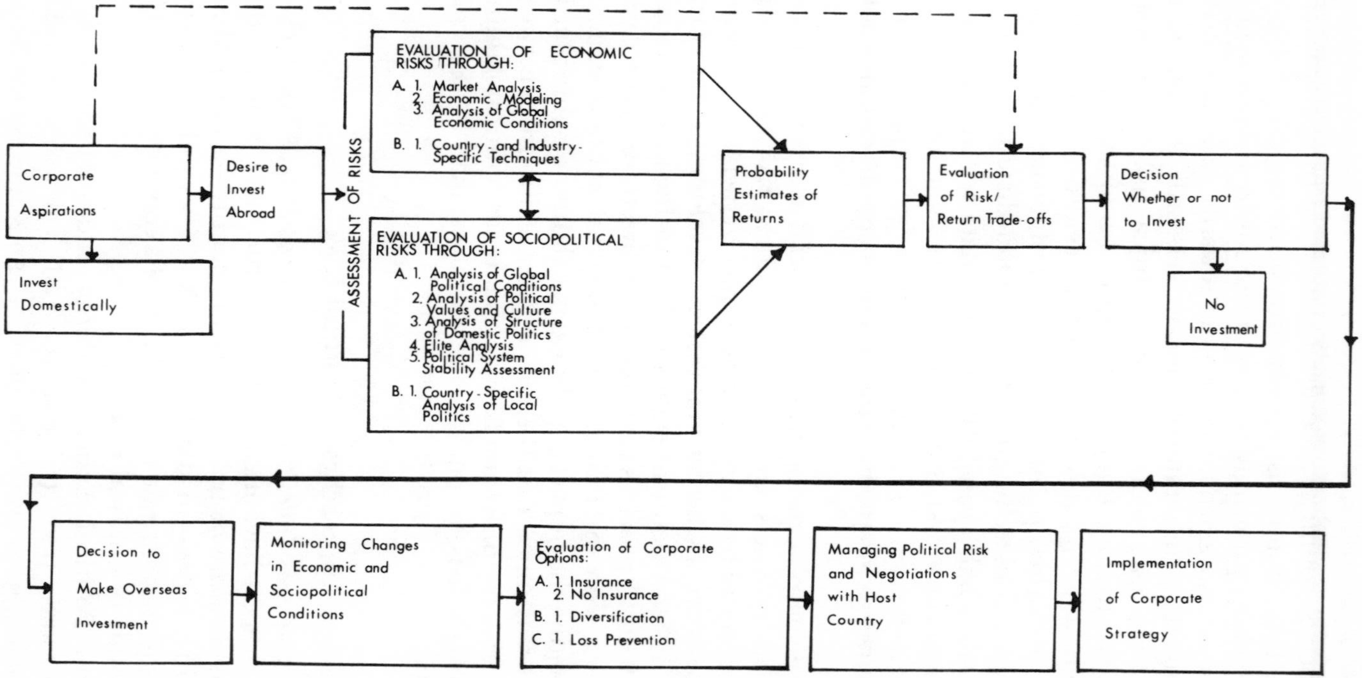

number of countries in order to ascertain comparative advantages. If so, it must use cross-national techniques.

Given the proven usefulness of various techniques of analysis in the measurement of economic rewards and risks, it is surprising that corporate decision-makers still rely on intuitive, top-of-the-head methods to assess political risk. Although several years ago Robock argued for specialized analyses of various components of political risk, there was no evidence of any systematic attempt to assess political risk in this fashion until quite recently. Social sciences techniques have two immediate advantages. First, they are usually based on empirical data selected and analyzed systematically and thus yield "harder" and more "objective" results. Second, it is often possible to employ forecasting techniques to predict the occurrence of certain political events.

The components approach and social sciences techniques of analysis to assess and measure political risk can perhaps be demonstrated by selecting an example. A crucial consideration in the decision of whether to invest in a developing country is often its long-term political stability. Two of the three risks against which OPIC provides coverage either directly or indirectly reflect concern with the host country's internal political stability. In evaluating the impact of political instability on political risk, it is usually assumed that there is a direct relationship between the two. Both the BERI and BI indexes include political stability and Stobaugh lists it among the variables that MNEs consider crucial.[17]

Integrated Approaches to Political Risk

In *Overseas Investment and Political Risk*,[18] Haendel, West, and Meadow have attempted to construct an empirical, indicator-based measure of political system stability—a Political System Stability Index—in sixty-five LDCs.[19] They did so primarily in order to demonstrate the feasibility of a components approach to the study of political risk.

The Political System Stability Index (PSSI) derives its importance from the role the political subsystem plays in establishing power relationships and norms for resolving conflicts in a society. It assumes that the degree of political stability in a country may indicate the society's capacity to cope with new demands.

Since direct measurement of all the characteristics of stability is impossible, an analyst must select and measure indirect indicators of these characteristics. The PSSI is composed of fifteen indirect measures of the political system's stability and adaptability.

The development of the PSSI is based on several considerations. First, rather than rely on "soft" opinion measures, such as the Delphi method, the PSSI uses quantitative measures based on "hard" data. Second, because of the complexity of the phenomenon being measured, the selected indicators must be amenable to being integrated with one another. Third, since observations averaged over a number of years yield more stable values than a single observation does, the indicators must be derived from available time-series data. Finally, the decision to use indirect forms of measurement requires that the indicators be selected and justified in terms of the PSSI itself.[20]

Because of the different considerations required to analyze political risk in the industrialized and communist countries, the PSSI is designed primarily for the LDCs. Data from the 1961-1966 period were gathered for three equally weighted indexes: (1) the Socioeconomic Index, (2) the Governmental Process Index, and (3) the Societal Conflict Index (see Figure 4.4). The PSSI is not a measure of the stability or tenure of a given regime or government. Rather, it is a much broader measure of the *system's* stability. Second, the PSSI is *not* based on the assessment of citizens' attitudes toward the stability of their political system, although indirectly it does attempt to measure these attitudes. Third, even though political stability may be viewed as a state of mind produced by the presence or absence of certain conditions in a given country, the PSSI is *not* based on intuitive judgments as to "underlying" latent instability. However, it does attempt to give some recognition to such subjective factors through the device of confidence estimates that accompany the PSSI index scores for each country. Finally, the PSSI is *not* flawless. In fact, it explicitly acknowledges the possibility of error. The confidence estimates provide a subjective estimate of its accuracy and reliability.

Table 4.2 presents the PSSI component score and confidence estimates for each of the sixty-five countries. The higher the PSSI scores, the greater the stability of political system; the lower the

Figure 4.4

FORMATION OF POLITICAL SYSTEM STABILITY INDEX (PSSI)

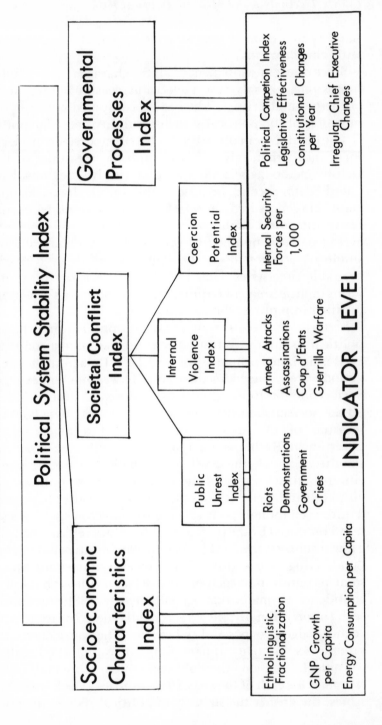

score, the lower the stability *relative* to that of the other countries. In each of the indexes, a positive score represents less social conflict, greater socioeconomic development, and greater stability with respect to the institutionalization of government processes. As Table 4.2 reveals, about half the countries show inconsistent patterns across the three PSSI components, with countries tending toward stability in one or two areas and toward instability in the remaining area(s). The remaining columns in Table 4.2 are the confidence estimates assigned to each of the component subindexes of the PSSI and an average confidence estimate calculated for the PSSI as a whole. Confidence estimates range from the high score of 1 to the low score of 5.

For easy reference the PSSI scores in Table 4.2 are ranked in Table 4.3. Since the scores are based on the 1961-1966 period, the results are intuitively very appealing. During that period, Zaire and the Dominican Republic were certainly among the least stable political systems. Zaire was racked by civil war and secessionist movements and at times appeared to be without a central government; the Dominican Republic experienced almost continual strife and turmoil, ranging from civil war and border clashes with Haiti to insurrections by Castro-backed guerrillas and U.S. military intervention. In contrast, in terms of rapid economic growth, level of development, and system of government, Israel certainly had one of the most stable political systems of the countries in our sample. Trinidad, inheriting a British parliamentary system, enjoying a healthy economic growth rate, and basking in the tranquility of Eric William's rule, was also quite stable.

However, in interpreting the PSSI scores and their associated confidence estimates, one should keep the following points in mind. First, all the scores are relative to each other, not to any country or countries outside of this sample. No attempt was made to make these scores comparable to the United States or developed states in general.[21] Since the PSSI scores are relative, a country with a score of +2.00 should be interpreted as being considerably more stable—not necessarily twice as stable—as a country with a score of 0.00. Second, it should be stressed that the PSSI seeks to measure system stability, *not* "democratization" or "Westernization." That both democratic Costa Rica and authoritarian Romania have almost identical PSSI scores should, therefore, not

TABLE 4.2

POLITICAL SYSTEM STABILITY INDEX (PSSI) WITH INDEX COMPONENT SCORES AND ASSOCIATED
CONFIDENCE ESTIMATES (1961-1966)

Country	Societal Conflict	Confidence (1-5)	Socio-economic Characteristics	Confidence (1-5)	Governmental Processes	Confidence (1-5)	PSSI	Average Confidence
Afghanistan	+.85	4**	-.57	3**	-.17	3	+.11	3.3**
Bolivia	-.67	3**	-.54	2	-.30	3	-1.51	2.7**
Brazil	+.20	2	+.41	2	+.11	3	+.72	2.3
Burundi	+.77	5**	+.39	3**	+.79	3**	+.37	3.7**
Cameroon	-.21	4**	-.90	3**	+.31	4**	-.80	3.7**
Central African Republic	+.85	4**	-.62	3**	-.45	3	-.22	3.3**
Chad	+1.23	4**	-.86	4**	+.04	3	+.41	3.7**
Colombia	-.47	2	+.51	2	+1.01	3**	+1.05	2.3**
Costa Rica	+1.20	2	+.37	2	+.87	3*	+2.44	2.3*
Dahomey	+.95	4**	-.51	3**	-2.25	3*	-1.81	3.3**
Dominican Republic	-3.26	3	-.45	2	-2.27	2	-5.98	2.3
Ecuador	+.04	3	-.49	2	-1.40	3	-1.85	2.7
Egypt	-1.04	3	+.94	3	-1.00	3	-1.10	3.0
Ethiopia	+.47	4**	-1.05	2	-.24	3	-.82	3.0**
Gabon	-.18	3	-.42	3	-.35	3	-.95	3.0
Ghana	-1.21	3*	-1.23	3*	-.79	3*	-3.23	3.0*
Greece	-1.08	3*	+1.58	2	+1.49	3**	+1.99	2.7
Guatemala	-1.42	3	-.12	3	-.58	3	-2.12	3.0
Guinea	+1.26	4**	-.27	3**	+.04	4**	+1.03	3.3**
Guyana	-.72	4	+.21	3**	-.55	3	-1.06	3.7**
Haiti	-1.19	3	+.45	4**	-.99	3	-1.73	3.3**
Honduras	+.17	3	-.19	3	-.30	2	-.32	3.0
India	-1.49	5*	-1.39	3*	+2.11	3	-.77	3.3*
Indonesia	-.72	4	-.68	4	-.52	3	-1.92	3.7
Iran	-.34	3*	-.31	2	+.04	2	-.61	2.7*
Israel	-.44	4*	+3.03	1	+1.97	3	+4.56	2.3*
Ivory Coast	+1.29	5**	-.41	3*	+.04	3	+.92	3.7
Jamaica	-.49	5**	+1.16	2	+.79	3**	+1.46	3.3**
Jordan	-.14	3	+1.66	2	-.10	3	+1.42	2.7

Kenya	-.02	4	-.62	3	+.15	3	-.49	3.3
Korea	-.28	4*	+1.47	2	-1.04	3*	+.15	3.0*
Liberia	-1.25	3*	-.63	3**	+.04	3	-1.84	3.0
Malagasy Republic	+.71	4**	+.38	3**	+1.42	3**	+2.51	3.3**
Malawi	+.56	4**	-1.49	3*	-.41	3**	-1.34	3.3**
Malaysia	-.23	3	-.08	2	+1.29	3**	+.98	2.7
Mali	+1.43	3**	-.77	3**	+.04	3	+.70	3.0**
Malta	-.82	3*	-.32	2	+.57	3	-.57	2.7*
Mauritania	+1.39	5**	-.03	4**	-.10	3	+1.26	4.0**
Morocco	+.05	3	-.78	3	-.24	3	-.97	3.0
Nepal	+.97	3**	-.74	3	-.47	3	-.24	3.0**
Nicaragua	+.07	3**	+1.13	4**	+.32	4**	+1.52	3.7**
Niger	+1.44	4**	-.69	4**	-.10	3	+.65	3.7**
Nigeria	-.27	3*	-.98	3	+.11	3	-1.14	3.0*
Pakistan	+.24	3	-.42	3	+.59	3	+.41	3.3**
Panama	-.52	3	+.95	2	+1.29	3**	+1.72	2.7**
Paraguay	-1.56	3*	+.17	3	+.32	3	-1.07	3.0*
Philippines	+1.13	3**	-.68	3	+1.97	3**	+2.42	3.0**
Romania	+.11	2	+2.52	2	-.10	3**	+2.53	2.3**
Rwanda	-.49	4**	+.24	5**	-.04	5**	-.29	4.7**
Senegal	+.77	3	-.58	4**	-.24	3	+.16	3.3**
Sierra Leone	+1.07	3**	-.74	4**	+.08	3**	+.11	3.3**
Sri Lanka	+.83	3**	-.77	3	+1.97	3**	+2.27	3.0**
Sudan	+1.20	3**	-.92	3	-1.18	4	-1.27	3.3**
Tanzania	+1.04	3	-.76	3	-.13	4**	+.31	3.3**
Thailand	+.82	3	-.06	3	-.10	3	+.88	3.0
Togo	-.16	4**	-.27	4**	-.31	3	+.24	3.7**
Trinidad	+.02	4**	+3.07	5**	+.79	4**	+3.70	4.3**
Tunisia	-.09	3	+.30	3	+.87	3	+1.19	2.7
Turkey	+1.09	3*	+.10	2	+1.28	2	+1.29	2.3*
Upper Volta	-.74	4**	-.62	3**	-1.02	2	-.55	3.3**
Venezuela	-.98	3*	+2.16	2	+1.42	2	+2.84	2.3*
Yemen	+.61	4**	+.39	4**	-2.89	2	-3.84	2.3**
Yugoslavia	-2.74	2	+1.02	2	-.10	3**	+1.53	2.3**
Zaire	-.74	5**	-.90	5**	-1.56	3	-5.20	4.3**
Zambia		4**	-.37	3	-.26	3	-1.37	3.3**

*It is estimated that PSSI score should be higher.
**It is estimated that PSSI score should be lower.

TABLE 4.3

POLITICAL SYSTEM STABILITY RANKINGS AND CONFIDENCE ESTIMATIONS (1961-1966)

Country	Score	Confidence	Country	Score	Confidence
Israel	+4.56	2.3*	Afghanistan	-.11	3.3**
Trinidad	+3.70	4.3**	Central African Republic	-.22	3.3**
Venezuela	+2.84	2.3*	Nepal	-.24	3.0**
Malagasy Republic	+2.51	3.3**	Rwanda	-.29	4.7**
Romania	+2.53	2.3**	Honduras	-.32	3.0
Costa Rica	+2.44	2.3*	Kenya	-.49	3.3
Philippines	+2.42	3.0**	Upper Volta	-.55	3.3**
Sri Lanka	+2.27	3.0**	Malta	-.57	2.7*
Greece	+1.99	2.7	Iran	-.61	2.7*
Panama	+1.72	2.7**	India	-.77	3.3*
Yugoslavia	+1.53	2.3**	Cameroon	-.80	3.7**
Nicaragua	+1.52	3.7**	Ethiopia	-.82	3.0**
Jamaica	+1.46	3.3**	Gabon	-.95	3.0
Jordan	+1.42	2.7	Morocco	-.97	3.0
Turkey	+1.29	2.3*	Guyana	-1.06	3.7**
Mauritania	+1.26	4.0**	Paraguay	-1.07	3.0*
Tunisia	+1.19	2.7	Egypt	-1.10	3.0
Colombia	+1.05	2.3**	Nigeria	-1.14	3.0*
Guinea	+1.03	3.3**	Sudan	-1.27	3.3**
Malaysia	+.98	2.7**	Malawi	-1.34	3.3**
Ivory Coast	+.92	3.7	Zambia	-1.37	3.3**
Thailand	+.88	3.0	Bolivia	-1.51	2.7**
Brazil	+.72	2.3	Haiti	-1.73	3.3**
Mali	+.70	3.0**	Dahomey	-1.81	3.3**
Niger	+.65	3.7**	Liberia	-1.84	3.0
Chad	+.41	3.3**	Ecuador	-1.85	2.7
Pakistan	+.41	3.3**	Indonesia	-1.92	3.7
Burundi	+.37	3.7**	Guatemala	-2.12	3.0
Tanzania	+.31	3.3**	Ghana	-3.23	3.0*
Togo	+.24	3.7**	Yemen	-3.48	3.3**
Senegal	+.16	3.3**	Zaire	-5.20	4.3**
Korea	+.15	3.0*	Dominican Republic	-5.98	2.3
Sierra Leone	+.11	3.3**			

*It is estimated that PSSI score should be higher.
**It is estimated that PSSI score should be lower.

be surprising. Moreover, since the PSSI has three components, strength in one component may compensate for weakness in the others in the final PSSI scores.[22]

A major purpose of the *Overseas Investment and Political Risk* study was to demonstrate the feasibility of constructing a quantitative tool to predict political system stability. The PSSI is based on the 1961-1966 period and, though dated, offers an opportunity to test the validity of the PSSI index. Unfortunately, however, no empirical analysis has yet tested the validity of the PSSI index by examining, say, the 1967-1974 period. The authors suggested that by looking at more recent events in these countries, the makeup of the PSSI can be adjusted. They also believed this process might yield an estimate of the confidence an analyst could have in using the PSSI as a forecasting tool.

According to Rummel and Heenan, "multivariate analysis" is what MNEs should use in order (1) to predict political trends based on present and historical data, and (2) to understand the underlying relationships that affect a nation-state.[23] They characterize the MNEs current approaches to political analysis as relying on subjective observations. They classify the current approaches as (1) the grand tour, (2) the "old hands" approach, and (3) the Delphi technique.

The grand tour relies on the ability of the firm's executives to observe and assess conditions in the area. As a result of receiving selective information and spending little time in the country, the executive may well recommend the adoption of plans that will yield catastrophic results for the company.

The "old hands" approach uses the expertise of experienced diplomats and others with an international background to examine political factors. The major flaw in such an approach is its reliance on the individual in charge of the evaluation. Quite often the individual selected may understand political affairs yet be incapable of bridging the gap between political events and their impact on business operations.

The Delphi technique depends on a panel of experts who evaluate the factors that concern the corporate decision makers. The drawbacks of this approach are (1) assuring an accurate and comprehensive list of the key political variables, and (2) establishing a reasonable means of combining the opinions of the experts into a single judgment.

Rummel and Heenan view political risk analysis as a multidimensional problem involving many political, economic, and sociocultural factors—the familiar trilogy. They argue that a country's political future is influenced by (1) domestic instability, (2) foreign conflict, (3) political climate, and (4) economic climate. These dimensions are further broken down into components. For example, the foreign conflict dimension is broken into (1) negative communications, (2) warning and defense acts, (3) intensity of violence, (4) negative sanctions, and (5) antiforeign demonstrations.

Rummel and Heenan apply their methodology to Indonesia and make the prediction (see Figure 4.5) that Indonesia's political instability will be a serious problem over the next five years. A major weakness of their methodology is its reliance on past data and its projection of future events. However, when combined with other qualitative and quantitative analyses, multivariate analysis may be of some assistance to the international business executive.

Nikkei Business has undertaken a very interesting effort aimed at ranking the investment appeal of fifty-three nations for Japanese enterprises.[24] This effort seeks to bridge the gap between political and economic investment considerations. The survey takes account of the different factors and reasons of investment appeal for a particular industry by classifying industries into market-oriented types as distinguished from resource and processing types. The factors chosen for assessing the market-oriented type of industry are: (1) political environment, (2) labor factors, (3) industrial infrastructure, (4) market environment, (5) foreign investment conditions, (6) external relations, and (7) relations with Japan. Each of the factors was weighted. For assessing the resources and processing type of industry, several factors and weightings were changed.[25] The results of this rating are given in Table 4.4.

Shell Oil Company's effort to assess and measure political risk is one of the most significant attempts to adapt political analysis for a corporation's overseas investment decisions.[26] Shell defines "political risk" as the "probability of maintaining an oil exploration/production contract which is perceived to be equitable to both host country and operator at the time of its being awarded, over a ten-year period, and in the face of changing

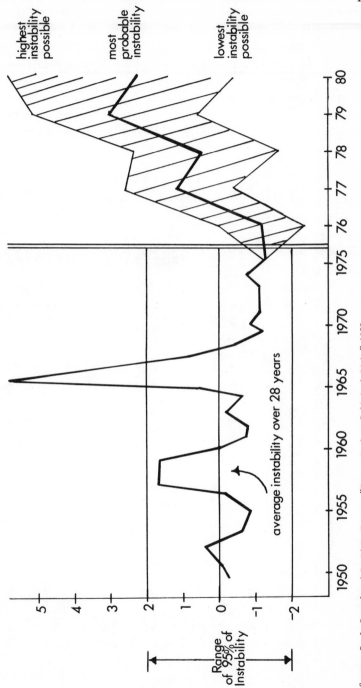

Figure 4.5
INDONESIA INSTABILITY

Source: R. J. Rummel and David A. Heenan, "How to Analyze Political Risk," 1977.
Published under the title "How Multinationals Analyze Political Risk,"
Harvard Business Review, January–February 1978.

115

TABLE 4.4

RANKING OF COUNTRIES BY INVESTMENT APPEAL*

A. MARKET-ORIENTED INDUSTRIES

Country	Ranking	Total	Political Situations	Labor Factors	Infra-structures	Market situations	Inviting conditions	External relations	Relations with Japan etc.
North America									
U.S.	AA	78.4	100.0	68.0	96.0	64.0	90.0	60.0	70.0
Canada	A	74.2	100.0	58.0	88.0	76.0	76.7	55.0	60.0
Latin America									
Mexico	B	66.6	66.0	66.0	70.0	64.0	73.3	65.0	60.0
Peru	C	60.5	66.0	56.0	40.0	62.0	66.7	60.0	64.0
Brazil	A	71.9	100.0	52.0	90.0	66.0	66.7	70.0	76.0
Argentina ...	C	55.4	33.0	64.0	66.0	36.0	86.7	60.0	50.0
Chile	D	52.9	66.0	64.0	36.0	38.0	80.0	45.0	44.0
Colombia	C	56.5	66.0	70.0	46.0	50.0	60.0	65.0	48.0
Venezuela ...	B	64.0	66.0	48.0	54.0	80.0	60.0	60.0	52.0
Bolivia	D	50.6	66.0	52.0	26.0	50.0	60.0	50.0	42.0
Costa Rica .	C	60.2	100.0	70.0	26.0	58.0	80.0	50.0	40.0
Puerto Rico .	A	68.2	66.0	40.0	30.0	50.0	90.0	50.0	58.0
Europe									
Britain	A	68.3	100.0	52.0	88.0	46.0	90.0	55.0	71.0
W. Germany .	A	75.2	100.0	82.0	88.0	66.0	86.7	65.0	64.0
France	A	75.0	100.0	63.0	98.0	70.0	80.0	60.0	60.0
Spain	B	64.4	66.0	56.0	84.0	64.0	73.3	65.0	34.0
Portugal	C	59.2	66.0	72.0	54.0	56.0	70.0	60.0	32.0
Belgium	A	71.8	100.0	52.0	62.0	70.0	90.0	60.0	54.0
Netherlands .	A	72.1	100.0	52.0	68.0	66.0	90.0	65.0	58.0
Sweden	A	67.9	100.0	50.0	82.0	60.0	86.7	60.0	54.0
Italy	B	64.2	100.0	48.0	82.0	60.0	73.3	55.0	30.0
Denmark	C	61.0	100.0	48.0	60.0	56.0	73.3	55.0	32.0
Austria	B	65.7	100.0	52.0	62.0	64.0	86.7	50.0	28.0
Finland	B	64.4	100.0	60.0	62.0	60.0	80.0	50.0	32.0
Norway	B	64.3	100.0	48.0	56.0	68.0	73.3	50.0	38.0

TABLE 4.4 (CONTINUED)

Switzerland	B	66.0	100.0	84.0	64.0	54.0	76.7	55.0	42.0
Ireland	A	70.1	66.0	58.0	34.0	54.0	100.0	55.0	45.0
Greece	B	66.4	100.0	66.0	38.0	62.0	80.0	60.0	54.0
Middle East									
Iran	C	61.9	66.0	46.0	40.0	72.0	73.3	65.0	62.0
Iraq	D	53.0	66.0	52.0	32.0	60.0	53.3	65.0	52.0
Saudi Arabia	B	66.8	66.0	46.0	44.0	70.0	90.0	60.0	62.0
Kuwait	B	63.3	66.0	62.0	28.0	80.0	73.3	50.0	40.0
Asia									
India	C	58.2	66.0	60.0	70.0	42.0	66.7	65.0	54.0
Pakistan ...	C	60.3	33.0	62.0	36.0	36.0	66.7	55.0	56.0
Thailand ...	B	65.7	66.0	78.0	40.0	62.0	73.3	70.0	88.0
Philippines	B	64.9	66.0	86.0	54.0	54.0	66.7	70.0	78.0
Malaysia ...	B	66.2	66.0	78.0	38.0	72.0	76.7	75.0	70.0
Indonesia ..	B	62.5	66.0	62.0	50.0	50.0	60.0	65.0	84.0
ROK	A	69.3	66.0	70.0	50.0	68.0	66.7	70.0	100.0
Hong Kong ..	A	75.1	100.0	80.0	42.0	74.0	90.0	65.0	80.0
Singapore ..	A	74.7	100.0	86.0	46.0	68.0	86.7	80.0	76.0
Africa									
Algeria	C	60.7	66.0	74.0	42.0	66.0	60.0	65.0	42.0
Egypt	C	58.0	66.0	64.0	44.0	60.0	73.3	45.0	34.0
Kenya	C	55.7	66.0	70.0	30.0	52.0	66.7	60.0	42.0
Zambia	D	49.2	66.0	80.0	26.0	40.0	53.3	55.0	38.0
Nigeria	B	62.9	66.0	58.0	34.0	74.0	56.7	70.0	57.0
South Africa	B	64.2	100.0	70.0	72.0	60.0	70.0	40.0	40.0
Tanzania ...	C	57.5	100.0	64.0	22.0	56.0	66.7	50.0	38.0
Ghana	D	46.8	66.0	58.0	26.0	40.0	66.7	35.0	30.0
Zaire	D	53.3	66.0	70.0	40.0	56.0	60.0	55.0	50.0
Sudan	C	55.2	66.0	52.0	24.0	64.0	66.7	45.0	40.0
Oceania									
Australia ..	A	73.9	100.0	60.0	82.0	68.0	80.0	65.0	69.0
New Zealand	B	66.9	100.0	64.0	56.0	58.0	83.3	50.0	58.0

TABLE 4.4 (CONTINUED)

B. RESOURCE AND PROCESSING INDUSTRIES

Country	Ranking	Total	Political Situations	Economic Situations	Infra-structures	Resources availability	Inviting conditions	External relations	Relations with Japan, etc.
North America									
U.S.	A	65.9	100.0	76.0	100.0	10.0	90.0	60.0	68.0
Canada	AA	83.2	100.0	76.0	92.0	100.0	76.7	55.0	60.0
Latin America									
Mexico	B	64.2	66.0	66.0	72.0	80.0	73.3	60.0	68.0
Peru	B	63.0	66.0	56.0	44.0	80.0	66.7	60.0	64.0
Brazil	AA	80.4	100.0	60.0	70.0	100.0	66.7	70.0	77.0
Argentina ..	C	54.9	33.0	40.0	62.0	40.0	86.7	60.0	50.0
Chile	B	64.3	66.0	34.0	36.0	100.0	80.0	44.0	44.0
Colombia ...	C	51.1	66.0	46.0	44.0	40.0	60.0	65.0	48.0
Venezuela ..	C	51.8	66.0	74.0	64.0	20.0	60.0	60.0	52.0
Bolivia	D	39.4	66.0	36.0	20.0	20.0	60.0	50.0	42.0
Costa Rica .	D	48.6	100.0	54.0	20.0	20.0	80.0	50.0	42.0
Puerto Rico	C	50.3	66.0	48.0	32.0	10.0	90.0	50.0	50.0
Europe									
Britain	B	60.3	100.0	52.0	94.0	8.0	90.0	55.0	70.0
W. Germany .	B	64.6	100.0	72.0	100.0	8.0	86.7	65.0	66.0
France	B	60.2	100.0	76.0	84.0	8.0	80.0	60.0	60.0
Spain	C	55.1	66.0	62.0	68.0	30.0	73.3	65.0	34.0
Portugal ...	D	44.3	66.0	54.0	44.0	20.0	70.0	60.0	32.0
Belgium	B	57.3	100.0	72.0	58.0	4.0	90.0	60.0	55.0
Netherlands	B	60.3	100.0	70.0	80.0	4.0	90.0	65.0	58.0
Sweden	C	55.4	100.0	66.0	64.0	10.0	86.7	60.0	34.0
Italy	C	51.7	100.0	64.0	78.0	2.0	73.3	55.0	30.0
Denmark	D	47.0	100.0	62.0	46.0	2.0	73.3	55.0	32.0
Austria	C	52.3	100.0	66.0	64.0	4.0	86.7	50.0	28.0
Finland	D	49.5	100.0	60.0	52.0	6.0	80.0	50.0	32.0
Norway	C	50.2	100.0	68.0	56.0	3.0	73.3	50.0	38.0
Switzerland	D	49.5	100.0	60.0	52.0	8.0	76.7	55.0	42.0
Ireland	C	51.6	66.0	48.0	34.0	10.0	100.0	55.0	40.0

TABLE 4.4 (CONTINUED)

Greece	C	50.8	100.0	58.0	34.0		80.0	60.0	54.0
Middle East									
Iran	A	73.5	66.0	72.0	64.0	100.0	73.3	60.0	62.0
Iraq	C	55.1	66.0	86.0	50.0	100.0	53.3	50.0	52.0
Saudi Arabia	A	76.2	66.0	60.0	56.0	100.0	90.0	60.0	62.0
Kuwait	A	69.5	66.0	70.0	48.0	100.0	73.3	50.0	40.0
Asia									
India	B	58.4	66.0	46.0	80.0	40.0	66.7	65.0	54.0
Pakistan	D	47.2	33.0	38.0	38.0	40.0	66.7	55.0	54.0
Thailand	C	55.8	66.0	60.0	30.0	40.0	73.3	70.0	88.0
Philippines	B	57.3	66.0	46.0	40.0	40.0	66.7	70.0	80.0
Malaysia	B	63.2	66.0	76.0	40.0	60.0	76.7	75.0	70.0
Indonesia	A	65.6	66.0	54.0	58.0	60.0	60.0	68.0	84.0
ROK	B	59.6	66.0	58.0	46.0	40.0	66.7	70.0	100.0
Hong Kong	C	54.2	100.0	62.0	32.0	2.0	90.0	65.0	82.0
Singapore	C	55.0	100.0	66.0	32.0	2.0	86.7	80.0	78.0
Africa									
Algeria	C	53.0	66.0	60.0	48.0	42.0	60.0	65.0	42.0
Egypt	C	52.5	66.0	68.0	40.0	42.0	73.3	45.0	34.0
Kenya	D	44.3	66.0	56.0	24.0	20.0	66.7	60.0	42.0
Zambia	B	59.4	66.0	42.0	24.0	100.0	53.3	55.0	38.0
Nigeria	A	69.6	66.0	66.0	50.0	100.0	56.7	70.0	56.0
South Africa	B	59.1	100.0	60.0	74.0	40.0	70.0	40.0	40.0
Tanzania	D	45.7	100.0	56.0	20.0	20.0	66.7	50.0	38.0
Ghana	D	48.6	66.0	42.0	26.0	60.0	66.7	35.0	30.0
Zaire	A	65.9	66.0	52.0	28.0	100.0	60.0	55.0	56.0
Sudan	D	41.9	66.0	52.0	22.0	20.0	66.7	45.0	40.0
Oceania									
Australia	A	76.9	100.0	72.0	86.0	70.0	80.0	65.0	68.0
New Zealand	C	56.5	100.0	58.0	48.0	28.0	83.3	50.0	57.0

*"Investment Appeal Rating of 53 Nations," The Japan Economic Journal, August 16, 1977.

economic and political conditions."[27] Thus, the political risk to a foreign oil company can take the form of (1) unilateral political actions taken by the host country to modify the original contract so that the corporation's operations in that country no longer yield an adequate return on the investment, or (2) host country acts that prevent or hinder the repatriation of either oil or funds.

Shell examined different approaches to political risk analysis. An analytical model based on time-series data was rejected because not enough research had been done on the linkage between political and economic events, on the one hand, and on their impact on U.S. corporations on the other. Shell's researchers also concluded that there was no readily available political risk assessment procedure developed by other companies that Shell could readily deploy.

Shell instead chose to form a panel of country experts from various disciplines who would "systematically assess the probabilities of specific adverse political actions facing a prospective Shell venture in a particular country."[28] This method of political risk assessment requires that (1) all panel members assess the same political and economic factors that could affect the enterprise, (2) the technique itself weigh and combine the panel members' individual assessments of the factors considered, and (3) the technique allow for communicating the panel's individual and combined assessments to the corporation's management. Shell's panelists provide their probability assessment concerning various propositions and state their confidence in that assessment. Furthermore, Shell's "panel of experts" method can make use of Bayes's theorem to update previous probability estimates upon the consideration of new information.

Once the responses have been compiled, the experts are given the results. They can then evaluate whether the quantitative assessment of their qualitative responses has correctly reflected their assessment of the uncertainties (see Figures 4.6-4.9). In addition, those experts who gave an opinion not in line with the majority view have the opportunity to explain their position.

The proponents of the "panel of experts" method argue that this approach provides a more realistic assessment of political risk. They also argue that it has such basic advantages as (1) neutralizing management's inherent subjective biases, (2) aiding in contract negotiations, (3) providing an "early warning

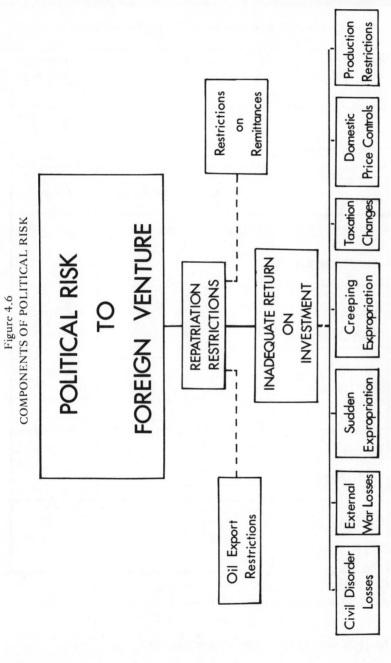

Figure 4.6

COMPONENTS OF POLITICAL RISK

Source: C. A. Gebelein, C. E. Pearson, and M. Silbergh, "Assessing Political Risk to Foreign Oil Investment Ventures," presented at the 1977 Society of Petroleum Engineers' Economics and Evaluation Symposium, Dallas, Texas, February 21, 1977.

122

Figure 4.7
POLITICAL RISK ANALYSIS–RESPONSE FORM

PROPOSITION:

1977 82=X
1982 87=✓

POLITICAL / ECONOMIC FACTOR:

GLOBAL SCENARIO: A B

CONFIDENCE / SUPPORT	WEAK	MODERATE	FIRM
STRONGLY SUPPORTING			
WEAKLY SUPPORTING			
NEUTRAL			
WEAKLY REFUTING			
STRONGLY REFUTING			

S ... R

COMMENTS
FACTOR BEHAVIOR (PRESENT AND FUTURE):

FACTOR INFLUENCE ON PROPOSITION:

Source: C. A. Gebelein, C. E. Pearson, and M. Silbergh, "Assessing Political Risk to Foreign Oil Investment Ventures," presented at the 1977 Society of Petroleum Engineers' Economics and Evaluation Symposium, Dallas, Texas, February 21, 1977.

Figure 4.8

PROBABILITY OF "TAXATION CHANGES" FOR COUNTRY X, 1977–1987

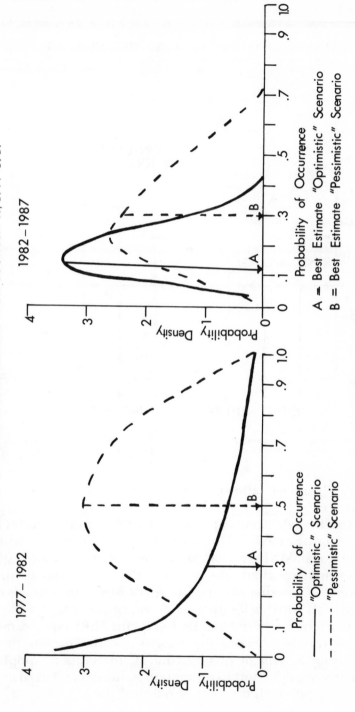

Source: C. A. Gebelein, C. E. Pearson, and M. Silbergh, "Assessing Political Risk to
Foreign Oil Investment Ventures," presented at the 1977 Society of Petroleum
Engineers' Economics and Evaluation Symposium, Dallas, Texas, February 21, 1977.

Figure 4.9
"TAXATION CHANGES"—1977–1982 "OPTIMISTIC SCENARIO"

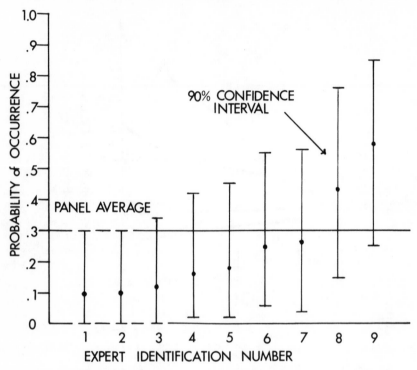

Source: C. A. Gebelein, C. E. Pearson, and M. Silbergh, "Assessing Political Risk to
Foreign Oil Investment Ventures," presented at the 1977 Society of Petroleum
Engineers' Economics and Evaluation Symposium, Dallas, Texas, February 21, 1977.

system," and (4) allowing for systematic cross-country comparisons.

Even though Shell's approach is subject to the criticism of simply being a modified Delphi technique, it has some instructive points for an MNE. Since an MNE's own executives formulate the issues and questions, the system will be developed with the purpose of meeting the specific needs of the firm. By dealing specifically with Shell's particular concerns, this approach avoids the much more general and far less useful BERI-type treatment. An MNE also chooses the experts for the panels, thereby exercising a form of quality control. In addition, simply by undertaking this effort a corporation is, in essence, forced to deal systematically with the issue of political risk.

Monitoring and Integrating Political Risk

Monitoring Political Risk

A major deficiency in the MNEs' conduct of foreign investment decisions lies in the monitoring of the investment environment *after* the decision to proceed with the initial investment has been made. Since no environment remains static, the issue becomes how to monitor a dynamic environment. In a dynamic political environment, such factors as changes, both actual and proposed, in laws and regulations affecting the enterprise, changes in party platforms, and changes in public opinion, to mention only a few, must be evaluated.

Bayesian analysis has been used by both private industry and at least one U.S. government agency to monitor political changes. In calculating the net present value of an investment, the analyst deals with expected values and prior probabilities. However, an analyst monitoring additional information may well seek to reflect these changes in terms of probabilities. Bayesian analysis can be used to revise the prior probabilities on the basis of additional information.[1]

Bayes's rule may be easier to visualize as a decision tree. Since many oil companies use this method in their exploration calculations, the following example is of an oil company that is considering drilling for oil.[2] Let us assume that the chief geologist thinks that the probability of a dry well (D) is 80 percent and the probability of finding oil (O) is 20 percent. The company can obtain more information through seismographic recordings. The evidence will be provided for one of three conditions:

Event R_1: no subsurface structure
Event R_2: open subsurface structure
Event R_3: closed subsurface structure.

Past experience reveals that the probabilities of these three events are 0.30, 0.36, and 0.34, respectively, if there is oil; and 0.68, 0.28, and 0.04, respectively, if there is no oil. The three possible outcomes of the test will yield a revised probability that there is oil at the site. The revised probability can be depicted as in Figure 5.1. Three applications of Bayes's rule are made:

$$P\ (O/R_1) = \frac{P\ (O \cap R_1)}{P\ (O \cap R_1) + P\ (D \cap R_1)} = \frac{.060}{.060 + .544} = .099$$

$$P\ (O/R_2) = \frac{P\ (O \cap R_2)}{P\ (O \cap R_2) + P\ (D \cap R_2)} = \frac{.072}{.072 + .224} = .243$$

$$P\ (O/R_3) = \frac{P\ (O \cap R_3)}{P\ (O \cap R_3) + P\ (D \cap R_3)} = \frac{.068}{.068 + .032} = .680$$

The first and third outcomes above would have a great effect upon the probability of finding oil. In assessing whether to undertake the exploration, therefore, it was important to find the probabilities of these three outcomes.

The CIA has adopted Bayesian analysis as one method of forecasting political events in the Middle East. Schweitzer describes how the CIA processes information by using Bayesian analysis.[3] Each analyst assigns probabilities to four scenarios or hypotheses that are of importance to the U.S. government. For example:

- No major hostilities are planned by Syria, Israel, or Egypt within thirty days;
- Syria, whether alone or in concert with other Arab states, plans to initiate major military action against Israel within thirty days;
- Israel plans to launch an attack against one or more Arab states within thirty days;
- Egypt plans to disavow the disengagement agreement within thirty days.

Figure 5.1:
BAYESIAN ANALYSIS

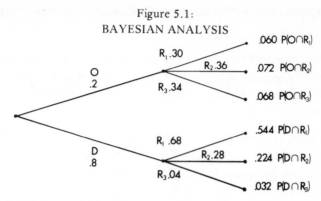

Source: Shiv K. Gupta and John M. Cozzolino, <u>Fundamentals of Operations Research for Management</u>, San Francisco: Holden-Day, Inc., 1974.

In dealing with the hypotheses that Israel is planning to launch a major offensive against Syria within thirty days or that Israel has no such plans, an analyst may assign the following probabilities:

- Probability that Israel is planning to launch a major offensive against Syria in thirty days—10 percent or 0.1.
- Probability that Israel is not planning such an offensive—90 percent or 0.9.

The following information arrives, and the question is how to treat it:

Israeli Finance Minister Rabinowitz stated that the nation's economic situation is "one of war and scarcity, not one of peace and prosperity." (Jerusalem Radio, 20 February, unclassified.)

An analyst may assign the following probabilities to this:

- Probability that this would be said if Israel is planning to launch a major offensive against Syria within thirty days—99 percent or 0.99.
- Probability that this would be said if Israel is not planning such an offensive—80 percent or 0.8.[4]

Bayesian analysis can be used to revise the probabilities of each

of the hypotheses based on this new information. The outcomes
are as follows:

- Revised probability that Israel is planning to launch a
  major offensive against Syria within thirty days—0.12.
- Revised probability that Israel is not planning such an
  offensive—0.88.

As more information is processed, the revised probability
becomes the prior probability for the purpose of assessing the new
information. Since each analyst translates the information into
probabilities, if the analysts disagree to a significant degree in
their probability assessment, the CIA will have them meet in order
to account for the differences.

Integrating Political and Financial Risks

MNEs can account for the economic and political risks of
overseas operations in several different ways. The most common
way to reflect the higher perceived risk is to raise the discount rate
for foreign investments.[5] The use of a shorter payback period
performs substantially the same function. But neither of these
methods provides a detailed examination of the risk involved or a
true reflection of the investor's fear. Accordingly, the use of a
higher discount rate will even out the investor's projected return,
even though the investor is aware that his expectations may be
quite to the contrary. However, by adjusting his cash flows
through the use of "expected values," the investor can focus on
the risks that are at the root of his concerns.

The differences in the methods used to integrate political with
financial risk analysis can be best illustrated by a relatively simple
example. Suppose the financial analysts of a firm have
determined that the cash flows for the project will be $50 million
for each of the next five years. They have arrived at this figure after
determining that there are three possible outcomes for the
periodic payoffs of this project. The probabilities are listed under
"Probability of Occurrence" in Table 5.1 and take account only of
the likelihood of financial success for the project, not of the
political risk. Stated another way,

$$E(A) = 0.10(\$20) + 0.20(\$30) + 0.70(\$60) =$$
$$\$2 + \$6 + \$42 = \$50 \text{ million.}$$

TABLE 5.1: EXPECTED VALUE

Probability of Occurence		Annual Payoff		Total
.10	x	$20 million	=	$2 million
.20	x	30 million	=	6 million
.70	x	60 million	=	42 million
		Expected value	=	$50 million

Therefore, the expected value of project A for each cash flow is $50 million.

In order to assess whether the project should be pursued, the firm can use net present value (NPV) analysis.[6] Assume that in addition to determining that the net *inflow* will be $50 million for each of the next five years, our financial analysts have also determined that the initial *outflow* or investment is $100 million, at no discount for the sake of simplicity. They have figured the discount rate r to be 10 percent, which takes account only of financial, not political, risk.

The NPV can be calculated as follows:

$50 million x 3.7908 = $189.54 million[7]
Therefore, the NPV = $189.54 million – $100 million = $89.54 million.

Using the present-value method, the proposal should be accepted because the net present value is greater than zero—in this example, $89.54 million.

However, many business executives are familiar with the process whereby the discount rate is increased dramatically for LDCs in order to take account of suspected political risks confronting the project. In fact, many firms have established a fixed discount rate for various LDCs. In order for a proposed project in such a country to be considered favorable, it may have to clear a discount rate as high as 45 percent.

In the example above, corporate executives may increase the discount rate to 30 percent in order to account for suspected political risks. Using the same figures except for the 30 percent discount rate, the net present value calculation is:

$50 million x 2.4356 = $121.78 million[8]

Therefore, the NPV = $121.78 million − $100 million = $21.78 million.

However, if corporate executives can more accurately analyze the political risk they fear, they can dramatically improve the political dimension of the overseas investment decision process. Accordingly, if the corporate executives in our case are in fact concerned with expropriation in Year 5 in reliance on a prediction that the project will be expropriated without compensation in that year, we suggest the following analysis: (1) allow the discount rate to reflect only financial evaluations, and (2) adjust the cash flow amount in order to reflect political risk evaluations.

Accordingly, the net present value calculation in our example would appear as follows:

$50 million x 3.1699 = $158.49 million[9]
The NPV = $158.49 million − $100 million = $58.49 million.

The difference in results between adjusting the discount rate and adjusting the cash flow amount is substantial: $21.78 million as opposed to $58.49 million. Furthermore, the method of adjusting the cash flow amount allows for greater explicit communications among corporate executives regarding the suspected political risk.

Bayesian analysis can also be used in an international business context to integrate political risk probability with expected value calculations. In our cash flow example dealing with the calculation of the net present value of a project, it has been assumed that the analyst's forecast of the political situation would not change. Furthermore, the probabilities listed under "Probability of Occurrence" took account only of the financial likelihood of success of the project; they did not take the political risk into account. Senior management, however, is concerned about expropriation or some other political event that may have an adverse impact on the future cash flow. The corporation's analysts may be bold enough to predict that the host country will not interfere with the enterprise during the first four years. However, they fear that in the fifth year, the host country may take steps against the project. Accordingly, we may be trying to predict whether the government will in fact expropriate the project without compensation in the fifth year. The analysts may predict as follows:

- Probability that the host country will expropriate in Year 5—40 percent or 0.4.
- Probability that the host country will not expropriate in Year 5—60 percent or 0.6.

Therefore, the expected value of the cash flow in the fifth year is $30 million.[10]

During the first two years of the project, however, the analysts have studied and evaluated many restrictive laws that affect the project. They provide the following probabilities:

- Probability that these laws would be passed if the host government is preparing to expropriate the project in Year 5—90 percent or 0.9.
- Probability that these laws would be passed if the host government is not preparing to expropriate the project in Year 5—40 percent or 0.4.[11]

The revised probabilities are as follows:

- Revised probability that the host country will expropriate in Year 5—60 percent or 0.6.
- Revised probability that the host country will not expropriate in Year 5—40 percent or 0.4.

Therefore, the revised expected value of the cash flow in the fifth year is $20 million.[12]

The major advantages in adjusting the cash flow amounts, rather than the discount rate, to reflect political risk can be summarized as follows:

1. When the discount rate is "adjusted," the effect is to "even out" the risk, even though that is not the decision-maker's

assessment of the future political conditions. In essence, it is the difference portrayed by the two cash flows discussed above, that is,

$$\frac{50}{(1.10)^1} + \frac{50}{(1.10)^2} + \frac{50}{(1.10)^3} + \frac{50}{(1.10)^4} + \frac{0}{(1.10)^5}$$

as opposed to

$$\frac{50}{(1.30)^1} + \frac{50}{(1.30)^2} + \frac{50}{(1.30)^3} + \frac{50}{(1.30)^4} + \frac{50}{(1.30)^5}.$$

2. Because adjusting the discount rate is easy and can be used to "fudge" without requiring explicit justification, the method advocated here—namely, adjusting the cash flow and having the discount rate reflect only the financial conditions—has the additional advantage of making the cash flow evaluation explicit, thereby allowing for greater communications concerning perceived political risk.

Bayesian analysis is not a panacea for MNEs that are increasingly concerned that the risks in the international investment climate outweigh the rewards. It focuses solely on the probabilities, or even more precisely, on changes in the probabilities. Furthermore, many corporate executives see the entire approach as too academic and too far removed from the realities of day-to-day business operations, even though several of the largest Fortune 500 firms use the approach. Implementing such an approach effectively within the corporation requires that certain executives systematically review and evaluate data. This takes time. Yet, despite these limitations, there are advantages to Bayesian analysis. In addition to the basic advantage of monitoring change, Bayesian analysis forces each analyst to indicate explicitly the *timing* as well as the *particular political event* that are at the source of his concern. By translating his concern into probability terms, each analyst must transform his subjective evaluation into a number. Since each analyst does so, the business executives are in a position to communicate regarding any discrepancies in their assessments. Such a process may well bring out information to which one member of the group was privy while the others were not. In short, it forces each analyst to assess new developments in terms of probabilities and their ultimate impact on the investment. The all too familiar corporate political risk assessment of "well, things are shaky, but . . ." or the all too common appendix on political conditions copied from the *World Almanac* and attached to a financial assessment of a project would be avoided and, one hopes, replaced by more sophisticated evaluations.

The quantification, monitoring, and integration of political risk with financial analyses also has the advantage of presenting information to corporate leaders in a more familiar format. This method does not in any way replace the importance of judgment. Rather, it simply forces these judgments to be made and stated systematically and explicitly.

6
The Management of
Political Risk

The management of political risk has recently emerged as an important issue in its own right. Among others, Margaret Kelly, Fred Greene and Bruce Lloyd have made substantial contributions to the subject of political risk management.

Political Risk Management

The subject of political risk management may be of assistance to corporate decision-makers who strive to formulate and implement alternative corporate responses based on the political environment the enterprise is likely to encounter. Risk management involves managing numerous risk situations and searching for the most efficient method of attaining the necessary protection. It entails identifying risks, assigning a value to them, anticipating losses, and making objective decisions about what steps to take before losses occur so that they have the least impact on the operation of the enterprise. It also includes a loss control program in order to help prevent or reduce the incidence or severity of losses.

The management of political risk includes the identification, analysis, and assessment of the risk as well as the responses formulated by the corporation on the basis of that assessment. Clearly, the corporation should implement procedures for getting the information it needs in order to make its decisions. Yet an MNE's decisions are likely to involve it in negotiations with both the host and home countries. Therefore, its political risk management effort should concentrate on adopting measures to insure a safe political environment in both the home and host countries, thereby assuring its own political viability.[1] Several of these measures have been mentioned in our earlier discussion of Kennecott Copper's strategy.

In order to cushion themselves against various types of risks, MNEs may not necessarily operate at their lowest cost as a result of integrating their production in the effort to neutralize the risk. For example, IBM uses its "interchange plan" in order to reduce the risk of becoming too dependent on production in any one country and the possibility of sudden expropriation or other negative acts affecting key production units. The plan calls upon IBM's World Trade Corporation to balance the manufacturing of the same components among several countries, so that if one source becomes unreliable, another can quickly replace it.

Margaret Kelly's view of corporate overseas investment is somewhat broader than Franklin Root's views. She argues that overseas investments are made in order to (1) develop foreign markets, (2) acquire tariff benefits or other forms of protection, (3) obtain lower costs, and (4) acquire raw material sources. Since political risk results from these foreign investment activities, Kelly's approach to political risk stresses risk management, whose purpose is to provide a systematic and analytical approach to selecting the best risk management technique. "The risk management process, in theory, is designed to assist in the performance of the risk management function."[2] Developing measures to treat the unique fundamental risks facing the foreign investor is simply a dimension of the risk management function. Kelly suggests that the basic risk management process for corporate decision making consists of "(1) the identification and analysis of loss exposure; (2) the measurement of losses associated with these risks; (3) the development of alternative techniques for treating each exposure; (4) the selection and implementation of the best technique or combination of techniques for treating each exposure; (5) the evaluation of results in an effort to improve the procedures of identification, measurement, and treatment."[3]

Kelly argues that indicators such as (1) the country's experience with self-government, (2) the extent of unemployment in the economy, (3) the equality of income distribution, and (4) the existence of constraints on social, economic, or political mobility can be used as indicators by which to judge a country's future political and economic stability. However, the broad nature of these categories, though of some benefit, is precisely their major shortcoming. Corporate managers must concentrate on those political issues, categories, or events that will affect, either favorably or adversely, their particular investment; general categories that are not custom-tailored and analyzed in terms of the specific corporation's exposure and risk will thus be of little benefit. Kelly attempts to bridge this gap by arguing that two factors form the basis of the loss probability estimate: (1) an evaluation of the local political, economic, and social conditions, and (2) the nature of the foreign investment. As for the nature of the foreign investment, Kelly points out, past experience indicates that the probability of unfavorable government action decreases markedly from extractive to manufacturing to retailing enterprises. Petroleum and other natural resource companies have been especially susceptible to political risk; foreign countries tend to feel that only nationals should be allowed to exploit basic resources.

Robock and Simmonds have suggested the following four steps, which differ slightly from Kelly's steps, for predicting political risk:

1. Understanding the type of government presently in power, its patterns of political behavior and its norms for stability.
2. Analyzing the multinational enterprise's own operation to identify the political risk most likely to be involved in a given area.
3. Determining the source of potential political risk.
4. Estimating the probability of loss and time span in which the loss may occur.[4]

In determining which policies and risks are acceptable to the MNE, senior management should strive to achieve the MNE's basic objectives. Accordingly, in order for the MNE to adopt a successful strategy, senior management should analyze corporate objectives through such fundamental questions as

1. What business are we in?
2. Why are we in it?

138 The Management of Political Risk

3. Should we continue to be in it, in the light of expected
developments in the technological, economic, political
and social environments in which we have to operate?
4. What business should we be in to ensure the long term
survival and development of the company?[5]

The first two questions can be considered before undertaking
political risk analysis, but the last two questions cannot. In fact,
the last two questions point to the importance of monitoring *after*
the decision to invest has been made.

An MNE should also examine its internal considerations and
determine the key commercial factors in order to evaluate its
capacity to undertake the investment. Once it has done this review
process, it can "begin to identify the way in which political
variables might affect the situation."[6]

Corporations are well aware that different industries have
different growth and strategic considerations—and are thus not
necessarily susceptible to the same political risk. Accordingly,
industries such as trading, raw material and extractive, service,
and manufacturing are affected differently by different political
events. In fact, a political event that may be disastrous for one
industry may not have any bearing for another and may be quite
advantageous for a third. Each firm should also consider its position and exposure within the particular industry.

Lloyd argues that foreign and domestic investment decisions
are essentially the same. However, he is quick to point out that
there are "a few more variables" in the foreign investment
decision process. But these additional variables are, in fact,
neither few nor simple. Indeed, Lloyd proceeds to list some of the
important differences in international operations.

1. the transmission of resources across the boundaries of
national sovereign states. . . .
2. the regulation of such transmission by governments,
3. the relations between the foreign company and host society
and its government,
4. the unpredictable nature of inter-government relations,
and
5. the substantial increase in the number of variables that
have to be considered, and the large number of new
risk factors that are not easy to quantify.[7]

In seeking to minimize its risks, an MNE should determine its objectives and its relationship with the host country. The determination of that issue will be of substantial assistance to an MNE in outlining its exposure. Determining its exposure, in turn, is an essential step in attempting to take the measures necessary to reduce the risk it confronts.[8] The MNE can examine its exposure through such means as a balance sheet or cash flow approach, depending on its accounting system and other considerations. Having determined its exposure, it should then establish which, if any, political events may affect each aspect of its exposure. The risk it faces will differ depending on such factors as its relations with the host country and unrest within the society.

A crucial reason for a firm's undertaking an internal audit of its overseas exposure to political risk is to adopt a strategy to cope with that risk. The traditional tools of risk management fall into the following six general categories: (1) avoidance, (2) transfer, (3) diversification, (4) loss prevention, (5) insurance, and (6) retention.[9]

Avoidance

A risk manager may recommend that the MNE not invest in a certain country if the probability of loss is too high. The option of diversification may also require some measures of avoidance. Thus, for example, a multinational bank that sets a limit or a ceiling on its exposure level in any given country is exercising both diversification and avoidance. It diversifies its loans by setting a ceiling on the exposure it allows per country. However, by establishing such a ceiling, it also refuses to consider those opportunities that arise once the country limit has been reached. Such a strategy is a modified avoidance, since even though the country itself has not been avoided as an area of investment, certain potential opportunities have been passed over.

Transfer

A risk manager may recommend that the MNE share the local enterprise with local investors or even with the host government itself. Other strategies, short of the transfer of some actual ownership to local interests, might include such measures as the hiring of high-level local managers and executives.

Diversification and Loss Prevention

For an MNE, a major reason for diversifying is to reduce the risk it faces. Accordingly, it may diversify in order not to be too dependent on a production facility or natural resource supply in any one country. By having facilities that can substitute for one another in numerous countries, it may be able to deter adverse actions by a host government. That is, it can point out during negotiations with the host country that it has readily available alternatives and will not be significantly affected by the host government's action. Furthermore, the host government may not have the necessary expertise readily available to take over the firm or the marketing capability to profit from its action. Both of these points can, of course, be made to the government. However, the MNE should carefully assess the dislocation costs associated with the host government's action.[10]

Insurance

A risk manager can recommend that the firm obtain insurance against political risk. We have dealt quite extensively here with investment insurance against loss from expropriation, inconvertibility, and from war, insurrection, and revolution. Insurance is also available against such political acts as ransom and kidnapping. In addition, export credit insurance is available against loss from the failure of foreign buyers to pay for goods and services. Exchange risk insurance is yet another type of political risk insurance that is available against loss from devaluation or revaluation of currency.

The purpose of insurance is to shield the firm's assets from unexpected losses—that is, to provide protection—although the insurance itself is only one means of attaining that goal. Securing "more insurance" is not necessarily the best way to get more protection. Risks can be transferred through insurance. However, the MNE should make this decision only after thorough review and examination, when it concludes that this is the appropriate course of action for it. It may decide to self-insure, in whole or in part, the risks it confronts. A higher deductible is one obvious way a company can assume a portion of the risk and thereby reduce the cost of the insurance, yet still retain sufficient insurance protection against the possibility of catastrophic loss. An MNE can also assume its risks through a self-insurance program by diverting the money earmarked for premiums into a separate fund to cover projected losses.

Retention

As any MNE can attest, not all political risk can be avoided, diversified, reduced, insured, transferred, or eliminated. The MNE that makes foreign investments will thus have retained, either through choice or necessity, the political risk it will face; in this case it becomes particularly crucial for the MNE's top executives to be able to reduce their perceived degree of uncertainty concerning political risk. In other words, top corporate decision-makers would, in such cases, prefer to have more confidence in the firm's political risk analysis. Accordingly, the techniques and methods of political risk analysis should be effectively used to reach a better basis for corporate decision making.

For its political risk analysis to be effective, the MNE must recognize, identify, measure, and predict potential political risk losses. It must examine the political risk in terms of its own objectives and functions. Furthermore, it should involve its executives in political risk evaluation. In addition, it can use a high-level staff group that has the confidence and cooperation of top management to undertake the unenviable task of analyzing the firm's political risk.

The selection of a meaningful risk-minimizing management policy is an extremely difficult task. Effective risk-minimizing policies have been developed for such particular risks as devaluation and exchange controls.[11] These policies have been aimed at reducing corporate exposure either well in advance or immediately before a predicted event. Although the success or failure of corporate responses to devaluation and exchange controls can easily be examined, it is much more difficult to link corporate management policies with the prevention of expropriation or damage to the firm's plant from political riots. Nevertheless, an MNE is likely to find that a careful consideration of the following questions may be instrumental in the development of the types of risk minimization effort it should undertake.

1. What level of profitability is expected? What level is acceptable?
2. Are current restrictions on the areas in which foreign investors are not allowed or discouraged likely to be extended to the firm's area?
3. Are there or will there likely be requirements to localize management or make stock available in the host country? Could the firm live with such requirements?
4. What pay scales are proposed? Would they tend to produce changes that would appear to challenge local values? Would "incentive" payments or a piecework system be offensive to the society?
5. What kind of relationship could be established with the local business community? Is local capital available to finance potential local partners? How much foreign exchange is required?
6. How great a gap exists between the host country's laws and its actual modes of operating? To what extent should the spirit, as well as the letter, of the law be followed by the firm?
7. What will be the net effect of the firm on the host country's pursuit of its national goals?
8. How important to the host country is any new technology the MNE can introduce?
9. Are the firm's products, personnel policies, and markets socially and politically acceptable to the host country?
10. Will the investment adversely affect the firm's operations, investments, or markets in rival countries? Are embargoes, boycotts, or government-induced harassment likely to result?
11. Is the tenor of nationalism in the country such that the firm's normal activities could be construed as destroying the nation's culture, challenging its fundamental values, or pillaging its national resources?
12. What local added value will the host country contribute to the product?
13. Relative to the size and wealth of the country, will the size of

the investment or the level of employment appear to suggest that the firm dominates or unduly influences the host government?[12]

Needless to say, these questions are intended to serve only as a guide. Many of the measures an MNE could take to reduce the types of risks it identifies are not likely to be implemented. However, an MNE operating in a host country where political events may have serious consequences for its exposure should consider the following actions:

1. Demonstrate through well-designed public relations efforts the importance of private and foreign investment to national development.
2. Avoid partisan involvement in local politics as much as possible, yet seek to identify the firm with national aspirations and objectives.
3. Stress the firm's contribution to the economy, especially by pushing exports.
4. Develop as strong a set of local suppliers, customers, and employees as possible.
5. Implement an effective training system for all levels of management.
6. Encourage local participation by using the local stock market or through joint ventures.
7. Seek to understand the way the government operates, the roles played by opposition elements, the distribution of wealth, and the sources of societal stability so that the points of leverage are clearly known.
8. Attempt to perform the maximum amount of research and development locally.
9. Try constantly to blend into the environment and become an integral part of society.
10. Seek to share the risk through the participation of an international agency.
11. Cultivate host country academics and intellectuals as sources of information and as potential governmental VIPs.
12. Develop a thorough understanding of the government and the political system.

13. Develop skills in dealing with government representatives.
14. Maintain up-to-date information on political and economic conditions.
15. Consider both public and private political risk insurance.[13]

An MNE's risk minimization strategy should also consider (1) devising particular risk minimization policies for risk exposure analyses, and (2) comparing the cost of appropriate risk minimization steps with the likely benefits and savings that such steps would yield.

In "Managing against Expropriation," David G. Bradley argues that not even revolutionary governments nationalize foreign investments indiscriminately.[14] He suggests that there is a rationale behind these governmental actions, a rationale the international executive must understand. Bradley assumes that a government's choice of which companies to expropriate is based on nonpolitical factors. He points to the increased importance of expropriation in view of his interpretation of statistics, which he claims show that the number of expropriations in 1975 was four times that of those in 1970 and fifty times those of 1961.

Although acknowledging the importance of specific political factors, he claims to present a "model for assessing the risks of nationalization."[15] But, even though Bradley presents some interesting findings and suggestions, he has certainly not presented a model. He suggests that international business executives should examine the historical rate of expropriation, both by region and by industry. They should then examine the firm's risk exposure in terms of (1) ownership, (2) technology, (3) vertical integration, and (4) size.

A regional analysis of expropriation since 1960 indicates that 49 percent of all expropriations occurred in Latin America, 27 percent in the Middle East, 13 percent in Black Africa, and only 11 percent in Asia.

Not surprisingly, Bradley has found that even though no industry is necessarily free from expropriation, certain industries are more susceptible to the danger than others. Extractive industries are the most sensitive to expropriation. A strong desire by Third World countries to control their raw materials accounts for the fact that "18 percent of all U.S. mining concessions and 12 percent of all U.S. oil properties were expropriated between 1960 and 1974."[16] The utility and transportation industries are also especially vulnerable to expropriation, having a 4 percent rate of expropriation. The manufacturing industry, however, has an extremely low 1.2 percent rate of expropriation. In this sector, the Sukarno regime in Indonesia and the Allende regime in Chile accounted for most of the expropriation.

Bradley finds that joint ventures with a host government have an expropriation rate ten times higher than a fully owned U.S. subsidiary. A joint venture with a local private partner, however, was found to reduce the risk of nationalization substantially; it also provides the major benefit of a local spokesman to press the firm's interests.

Advanced technology can provide a substantial barrier to the danger of expropriation. IBM, for example, has not experienced one expropriation during the past sixteen years, even though it has operations in 127 countries; one of the major reasons for this is that an LDC host government would be unable to operate an expropriated IBM company. Corporations facing the highest rate of expropriation are those in the middle range of technology, apparently because low-technology companies, such as textiles, do not arouse the interest of host governments.

A vertically integrated MNE faces a lesser chance of expropriation because of the control it exerts over either the supply sources or the marketing distribution of its subsidiary. A plant that cannot operate independently of its parent company is of little benefit to the host government.[17]

Bradley also points out that the rate of expropriation is much higher for companies with over $100 million in assets than it is for companies with assets under $1 million. A host government may not feel that an enterprise of small value is worth the problems that may follow upon expropriation. In addition, the larger the investment, the greater its visibility and stigma of foreign ownership.

Based on his research, Bradley suggests five possible strategies to lessen the MNE's risks in foreign investments:

1. Seek joint ventures with local private parties.
2. Concentrate proprietary research, product development, and process technology in the United States. . . .
3. Ensure that each new investment is economically depen-

    dent on the parent corporation in the United States. . . .
 4. Avoid local branding. Establish a single, global trademark
    that cannot easily or legally be duplicated by an expropriat-
    ing government. . . .
 5. Adopt a low profile, multiplant strategy, with a number of
    small investments spread throughout several countries.[18]

Negotiations with Host Governments

As American and European MNEs have expanded their
investments in Third World countries, corporate executives
have become increasingly involved in negotiations with foreign
government officials. These negotiations deal with new foreign
investments as well as with host government demands for
modifications of contracts covering existing investments.

Third World countries have become increasingly sophisticated in their negotiating stance with MNEs. Many have
begun to employ social cost/benefit analysis to screen foreign
investment proposals and to monitor those projects already
in operation.[19]

The MNE seeks to minimize its early costs and maximize later
benefits; the host country, in contrast, attempts to maximize early
benefits and minimize later costs. The following example is
particularly instructive because the host country is not an LDC.
Raytheon, the American electronics firm, was attracted to Sicily
both by low wages and by readily available capital. The Italian
government offered Raytheon an attractive tax incentive to build
the plant in Sicily. Once the initial investment had been made and
operations had begun, however, the government increased the
taxes. Since the higher tax rate discouraged other investors from
entering the region, the government had to increase taxes even
further in order to pay for such public goods as new roads,
schools, and utilities. As a result, Raytheon shifted its production
to a plant in France and laid off a very large number of Sicilian
workers. The mayor of Palermo then occupied the Raytheon
plant. The Raytheon subsidiary declared bankruptcy and
repudiated a number of unsecured obligations that local banks
had provided. A regional economic crisis ensued, and Raytheon
decided to auction off the plant. However, the situation had become so serious that the Italian government announced that a

nationalized Italian company would take control of the plant. This development had the effect of discouraging foreign electronic investments in Italy.

Third World countries in need of foreign investment are likely to offer many incentives in order to attract it. Their perceptions of the benefits that accrue to their economies usually outweigh the social and economic costs they associate with the investment. An MNE can provide a Third World country with such benefits as technology, capital, and access to markets.[20] As the project becomes increasingly profitable, the MNE is likely to repatriate its profits and may decrease the infusion of new technology and capital. The host government will place increased demands on the foreign corporation to renegotiate and change the terms governing the investment. Even though the MNE will consider its project a major and continuing contribution to the local economy, the host country is very likely to view its need of the foreign firm as rapidly declining over time. If the foreign investor refuses to yield to such host government demands as a greater role for local managers and increased tax payments, the host government may consider the drastic option of expropriation.

The relative bargaining positions of the MNE and the host government also change over the time span of the investment.[21] Before the investment, a host government is likely to make the concessions necessary to attract the investor. The MNE is in a strong bargaining position because it may have the realistic option of investing in other countries. The government wants to obtain such resources as technology and capital from the MNE; the MNE still can seek the resource in that particular host country or turn to a different investment environment. But once the investor has developed its project in the host country, the host government may want to consider whether the investment should be allowed to continue. If it decides that the project is needed, it will seek to determine what steps it should take to maintain the investment. Therefore, after the investment has been made, it is likely to be in an improved bargaining position vis-à-vis the MNE. If the MNE rejects the host government's demands, it may find the resulting cost unacceptable in light of the investment it has already made.

Despite the shift in the relative power positions of the host government and the MNE, the MNE may be able to take steps to prevent, or at least slow down, this shift. It may be able to maintain its leverage with the host country through the latter's continued dependence on it for such factors as new technology and skilled managerial personnel. Therefore, in order to prevent injurious actions by the host government, the MNE should seek to maintain its ability to retaliate against the host government. Rather than threaten the host country with such a possible exercise of power, the MNE may prefer to demonstrate to the host government that its continued presence and operations in the country are of significant benefit to the society. Many of the steps suggested by Bruce Lloyd are in essence designed to assure the continued maintenance of the MNE's leverage on the host government. Such measures as maintaining the dependence of the subsidiary in the host government on the parent company for technology and access to world markets will provide the host government with reasons to pause and reconsider any adverse actions aimed at the firm.

Since the relationship between the MNE and the host country will be dynamic, the MNE should be willing to change the terms of the original agreement. The original contract is likely to have been negotiated at a time when the MNE was at the height of its power vis-à-vis the host country. Even though most foreign investment contracts have clauses that seek to provide stability over a long time period, host countries often demand the renegotiation of contracts. The investor may feel that he has an absolute legal right to rely on the "sanctity of the contract." However, once the host country is aware of the success of the project, it may begin to press for the renegotiation of the agreement. Since the host government's bargaining position has also improved once the investment has already been made and operations initiated, the MNE may be well advised to renegotiate certain provisions, especially those pertaining to taxes.

The investment environment does constitute a dynamic and often puzzling situation for the investor. However, if the MNE maintains its leverage on the host government through such measures as access to markets, new technology, and capital, it is not likely to be subject to the types of host government actions that will force it to terminate its operations. Those foreign investments the host government no longer considers essential face the greatest danger of survival in the host country. Therefore, the MNE should intermittently assess its leverage on the host government and attempt to make certain that the host country benefits and clearly perceives those benefits that the MNE's operations provide the society.

Despite the political risk an MNE takes in its overseas operations, it need not feel completely helpless. Through risk management techniques and negotiations with the host country, it can seek to establish and maintain the "rules of the game." It must be careful not to take actions toward the LDCs that will result in self-fulfilling prophecies with harmful consequences to the enterprise. Accordingly, it must balance its interests with the demands of LDCs. However, not even the most radical host government could expect an MNE to invest in a foreign subsidiary and maintain that investment if the operation does not meet the required threshold of profitability.

Conclusion and Summary

Because of their power, function, conduct, and visibility, multinational corporations have come under considerable attacks from many sources.[1] By the early 1970s direct foreign investment, primarily by MNEs, was rapidly replacing trade as the major factor in international economics. In fact, MNEs, 50 percent of which were American-based, accounted for about 20 percent of the world's goods and services. U.S. multinationals also produce overseas five times the amount of U.S. exports. Yet despite, or perhaps because of, this growth, MNEs have come under increased pressure from home and host governments in such areas as taxation and regulation.

Many observers regard the MNE as the catalyst for economic development in the LDCs. Several have assumed that there will be a significant transfer of manufacturing industries and technology from the industrialized countries to the LDCs.[2] Yet a recent market survey indicates that U.S. companies have been reducing their plans for new investments in the developing countries. Henry Kissinger has stated that "transnational enterprises have been powerful instruments of modernization both in the industrial nations, where they conduct most of their operations, and in the developing countries where there is often no substitute for their ability."[3] However, MNEs have limits on their power, as the seizure of many corporate assets shows. But the risk management practices of several MNEs have deterred host governments from expropriating the foreign subsidiary. An MNE has the ultimate recourse of ceasing operations in a host country if the government's demands are unacceptable. However, there are costs associated with such a step, and they may be too high for the MNE. Interestingly enough, even though U.S. direct foreign investment in the LDCs has declined during the past several years, U.S. exports to LDCs have increased substantially—from about $10 million in 1968 to some $40 million in 1976.

MNEs operating in the present era of low economic growth are likely to feel a substantial impact from political factors affecting their earnings and overall corporate strength. Therefore, they should analyze political risk whenever governmental action or some other political event can change the outcome of a commercial decision. Since the line between political and commercial risk may in fact be blurred at times, the management of the political risk aspect may be particularly troublesome. However, whether political risk is analyzed as a separate phenomenon or treated as part of the overall investment analysis, the crucial point is that it be identified and evaluated both explicitly and systematically.

In seeking to analyze, assess, and manage political risk, an MNE should be interested in those political disruptions that affect its investment and operations or those political events that provide it with opportunities. One firm has adopted a "systematic approach" to political risk analysis by determining priorities that reflect the broad areas of political risk it faces. These priorities are (1) nationalization or expropriation, (2) social and political unrest, (3) stringent contractual obligations, (4) negative government policies and tax laws, (5) stringent currency controls, and (6) labor unrest. It also correctly determined that a complete assessment should also include an in-depth analysis on an individual country/project basis. Finally, it appreciated the need for inputs from various departments within the firm and for cooperation among these units to facilitate a smooth flow of information.

However, a bank that statistically ranks countries by economic, financial, and political measures may use them for the purpose of providing a first-cut analytical evaluation of a country's creditworthiness and outlook for economic growth relative to other countries. One major regional bank uses this approach combined with a consideration of other factors as a check on the intuition and judgment of other bankers and analysts.

Because the assessment of political risk may be in large part a matter of perception, the factor of subjectivity is extremely important in international business, where corporate managers must evaluate the events and conditions in a foreign host country. Since their estimate of political risk is likely to be biased as a result of subjective factors, which cannot be totally eliminated, international corporate executives should at least try to be aware of their bias.

Quantitative studies of political risk tend to concentrate on instability, even though political instability has not been definitively shown to be directly related to business losses or gains. Furthermore, these analyses use aggregate data, although political risk should also be viewed from the perspective of a particular project, a particular firm, or, at least, a particular industry.

As surveys of international business executives indicate, erroneous perceptions of overseas opportunities can still provide an obstacle to investments in certain countries. In fact, because of the overriding importance attached to political risk, many corporations will avoid certain countries, or even regions, because of political considerations.

A study conducted for The Conference Board has found that MNEs (1) pay very little attention to political assessments, (2) do most of their political analysis during their entry or exit from the host country, (3) do not attach sufficient importance to political intelligence at the corporate headquarters level, and (4) do not sufficiently integrate political assessments with the overall corporate decision-making process.[4]

During the past several years, terrorism has become of significant concern to international business.[5] The numerous kidnappings and murders of international business managers in Argentina as well as the kidnapping and murder of a leading industrialist such as Hans Martin Schleyer indicate that terrorism poses a serious danger in many societies. The Red Brigades in Italy have focused their terrorist attacks both on political leaders such as Aldo Morro and on business leaders. Furthermore, Italy's Red Brigades have labeled U.S. multinational corporations as their major enemies.

The incidence of terrorist attacks aimed at foreign businessmen in several industrialized countries demonstrates quite dramatically that political risk is not limited to LDCs. In fact, the political risk dimension is likely to become increasingly important for investment decisions in the industrialized countries as well. As noted earlier, the fact that we did not explicitly deal with political risk analysis for industrialized countries in no way implies that these countries are immune from political risk. In France, for example, the hostility toward big business seems to run deep. A survey taken during the French 1978 elections indicated that a majority of the French population supported the pledge by the leftist parties to nationalize several major corporations.[6]

MNEs invest overseas primarily in order to capture a foreign market, acquire natural resources, or exploit lower production costs. Since they do not invest in a country simply because of its safe political conditions, political risk insurance is itself not an incentive for U.S. foreign investment. Nevertheless, MNEs may forgo certain foreign investments—despite their economic and financial attractiveness—because of an unacceptable political risk. Therefore, political risk insurance may neutralize the risk.

The recent congressional restrictions placed on OPIC are likely to increase the important role of the private insurance industry, notwithstanding the failure of the "privatization" effort. The dramatic expansion of the private insurance coverage provided by such companies as Lloyd's of London and American International Group seems to indicate that certain insurance companies are willing to shoulder more political risk. Coverage is available for such political risks as hijacking, war, strikes, riots, and kidnapping. Lloyd's has insisted on global coverage for its corporate clients and has not written policies limited to investments of extremely high exposure.[7] The private insurance industry has sought to complement, rather than compete with, various national insurance programs. However, the private insurance industry has a significant advantage over national insurance programs in terms of writing policies that are custom-tailored to the investor's needs.

The purpose of this volume has been to examine political risk analysis and management. We have sought to do so by examining both the role of MNEs in Third World countries and the role of the U.S. government in this relationship. Although OPIC's authorization has been extended, the congressional restrictions placed on it indicate that U.S.-based MNEs will have to bear a rapidly increasing political risk burden.

Through a review of much of the literature on political risk, we have attempted to clarify the concept of political risk. In addition, we have highlighted the importance of securing political information and integrating it with financial analyses. We have also reviewed a number of recent approaches for analyzing and quantifying political risk. Some of these approaches are currently being sold to MNEs as a "service." We have argued quite strongly for formation of custom-designed political risk analyses by MNEs through the utilization of an in-house capacity.

Furthermore, we have sought to examine various risk management tools and have advanced a possible approach for monitoring political risk and a way to integrate political and financial analyses.

The forecasting of political risk will remain little more than educated guesswork until reliable measures of political risk are developed and tested. Data are available from the AID/OPIC experience, but very little has been done to determine the patterns of those events.

The Political System Stability Index (PSSI) was developed by using data for the 1961-1966 period. Originally, it was to become a forecasting instrument, that is, it was to be compared to data on what actually occurred during the 1967-1973 period. If necessary, its indicators could be replaced or adjusted to best "fit" the reality of those years. An adjusted PSSI could be constructed for a period and used as the basis for making forecasts about subsequent periods.

For every other component that a political risk analyst deems relevant, a similar procedure could be followed until a complete picture of the political risk an investment faces is drawn. Figure 7.1 illustrates the types of indicators for which a components approach might also be appropriate. The method developed by the Shell Oil Company also begins with a components model but seeks to quantify expert opinion and thereby determine political risk.

The PSSI and Shell examples illustrate a components

Figure 7.1
LEVELS OF ANALYZING POLITICAL RISK

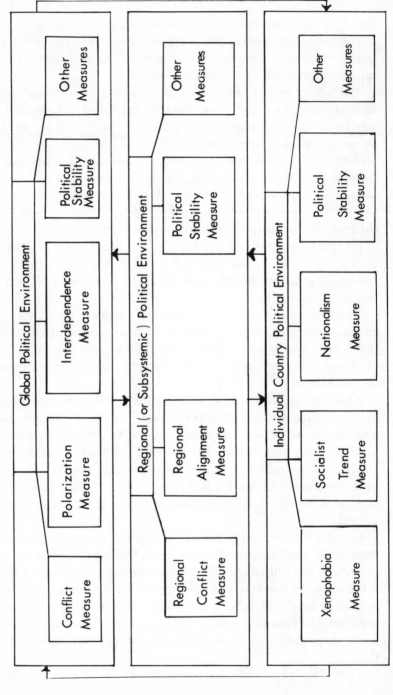

approach to the measurement of political risk. To compile a comprehensive estimate of the political risk for a particular investment, MNEs should consider incorporating the estimates of risk from many sources and levels in the environment.

The scope and breadth of a political research effort will depend on such factors as the MNE's capacity to expend its resources on this effort and the degree of its overseas exposure. This research effort should use a mix of quantitative and qualitative analyses depending on the type of risk that is being examined.[8] By undertaking explicit and analytic political risk research, MNEs are likely to feel that they are examining the risk factor. By undertaking explicit and analytical political risk research, they are likely to feel that the risk factor is being determined more accurately, which will provide the additional benefit of reducing their uncertainty.

Since the corporate cost of not monitoring political risk is likely to increase in the future, MNEs should establish an in-house capacity to analyze and manage political risk. This in-house corporate staff should begin by developing a model for its political risk analysis, for a corporate model is essential to the formation of a custom-tailored political research effort. Such a model also serves such useful purposes as aiding in the processing of information and providing a framework for establishing a relationship between political events and the firm's welfare. Senior management should encourage the development of a corporate capability to undertake political risk research. They should be sensitive to political factors and encourage the systematic integration of political factors into the corporation's investment decision process and maintenance of its overseas investment.

Appendixes

APPENDIX A:
A Political System Stability Index

Social scientists tend to view society as a system of relationships and patterns and interactions that are directed toward the achievement of certain goals, such as economic progress, political stability, or social harmony.[1] To achieve these various goals, distinct yet interdependent subsystems arise in all societies. Each subsystem is geared to accomplish specific societal goals; for example, the economic subsystem may be viewed as those societal interactions relating to the allocation of scarce resources and to the means of production and distribution.

The political system is the most important subsystem in a society, since it not only defines the parameters of the other subsystems but also provides the necessary stability for the others to function. In a sense, the political system may be viewed as the arbiter governing the performance of the other subsystems in order to meet social needs. The stability of the political system at any moment is directly related to its adaptability to a constant barrage of conflicting internal and external demands. The political instability that a society manifests may be viewed as an indication of its inability to cope with new demands made on it or its inability to move to a new functioning equilibrium.

The PSSI data were collected for a sample of countries, selected from the official OPIC country list of April 1974. The sample was composed of sixty-five of the sixty-nine countries for which OPIC insurance was then under review or available. Lack of appropriate data required the deletion of some countries from the sample. Most of the countries dropped were not independent countries during the period for which data were collected, 1961-

1966.[2] The sample contains the overwhelming majority of LDCs, with very small countries constituting the most notable omissions. Most of the LDCs of concern to investors are included in this sample.

Consideration was given to extending our sample to the industrialized countries of Western Europe, Canada, Japan, Australia, New Zealand, and the remaining communist states. But the communist group of countries was excluded because of the low likelihood of significant U.S. investment in them in the near future, but more importantly because of the very different political considerations involved in such investments. The noncommunist developed states were excluded for two reasons. First, much material and many analyses on the socioeconomic and political conditions in these countries are already available. Second, because of the scoring method employed (Z-scores), the inclusion of these developed countries would have skewed the scores of the LDCs, reduced the variance among them, and hence distorted the PSSI scores.

Over twenty-five indicators were initially considered for inclusion in the PSSI, and even more methods of organizing, ordering, and scoring these variables were appraised before constructing the index based on fifteen indicators. The PSSI is composed of three equally weighted indexes, all of which include indicators that bear on the stability of the political system: (1) the Socioeconomic Index, (2) the Governmental Processes Index, and (3) the Societal Conflict Index. The first two indexes are composed, respectively, of three and four equally weighted indicators. The Societal Conflict Index was constructed from three subindexes: the Public Unrest Index, the Internal Violence Index, and the Coercion Potential Index. For reasons noted below, the Public Unrest Index was given a weight of 0.2, and each of the other two subindexes was given a weight of 0.4. Data for each of the fifteen basic indicators were collected from various sources and averaged for the five-year period 1961-1966. Since the measurement scales used in scoring the indicators were not comparable, the raw data were standardized (Z-scored) so that the indicator scores were additive. Whenever necessary, the component indexes were also standardized.

Four criteria governed the selection of indicators. First, data on the indicator had to be available for the six-year period across the overwhelming majority of our countries. Second, only indicators whose theoretical value had been demonstrated in other studies of political stability were chosen. Third, indicators that tapped different facets of political system stability were sought; that is, attempts were made to minimize indicator overlap. Finally, since comparability across countries was required, only indicators that were appropriate for the vast majority of countries under consideration were selected. Strong arguments can be made against the inclusion of certain indicators for selected countries. Nonetheless, after considering the appropriateness of many other assumptions about stability, of many other indicators of stability, and of different weighting alternatives, we concluded that these fifteen indicators, structured as outlined in Figure 4.4, represent the best configuration of indicators for this sample of LDCs. Moreover, the broadness of the indicator base suggests a higher probability that random errors across the indicators will cancel each other out, resulting in a composite score that is more reliable than the score of any one or any group of the indicators.

Since the scores were standardized with a mean of zero and a standard deviation of one, the component scores represent distances from the mean of all countries for each index. The PSSI component scores are summated distances from the zero means.

Since the components are equally weighted, a country with a particularly strong tendency toward stability in one area will be balanced by any tendency toward instability in other areas. For example, India's score is a product of high negative Social Conflict and Socioeconomic scores and a high positive score on the Governmental Processes Index. Zaire has a very high negative Social Conflict score and negative Socioeconomic and Governmental Processes scores; as a result, it has a very low or negative PSSI score.

Where it could be ascertained that a component score should be higher (*) or lower (**) than it was, an indication was attached to this confidence estimate. Confidence estimates ranged on a scale from 1 to 5:

1—Very high confidence in the accuracy, reliability, and comparability of the score to those of other countries.

2—High confidence in the accuracy and reliability of the score. A few doubts as to the comparability of the score to those of other countries due to missing data, under-reporting, or overreporting of events.

3—Moderate confidence in the accuracy and reliability of the score. Some doubts about the comparability of the score dur to missing data, underreporting or overre-porting of events.

4—Low confidence in the accuracy and reliability of the score. Serious doubts as to the comparability of the score due to missing data, underreporting or overre-porting of events.

5—Minimal confidence in the accuracy and reliability of the score. Very severe doubts about the comparability of the score due to missing data, underreporting or overreporting of events.

Confidence estimates were assigned to index scores on the basis, in part, of nonarbitrary factors, such as the existence of missing data. Where data were missing for an indicator, the Z-score mean of zero was assigned. Although data were missing for only a few countries on certain variables, this was taken into consideration in the assignment of confidence estimates. In large measure, nevertheless, these estimates were based on the authors' evaluation of the scores and their knowledge of these countries.[3]

The Component Indicators of the PSSI

The socioeconomic component of the PSSI consists of three indicators. The first is a measure of ethnolinguistic fractionaliza-tion based on a country's ethnic and linguistic heterogeneity.[4] High fractionalization suggests the existence of fundamental social cleavages and a considerable potential for civil strife. Conversely, the lower the fractionalization, the lower the likelihood of civil strife. Since the existence of important ethnic and linguistic minorities may suggest latent conflict, ethno-linguistic fractionalization is an important indicator of the current strain and potential instability of a political system.

The other two indicators composing the Socioeconomic Index

are percentage growth in GNP and energy consumption per capita.[5] Percentage growth in GNP and growth in energy consumption serve as indicators of a developing country's ability to satisfy the economic demands of its citizenry. Percentage growth in GNP is also an indicator of the ability of the political system to provide a favorable political climate in which the economy can expand. "Relative deprivation" theorists such as Gurr[6] and Tanter and Midlarsky[7] have shown that a falling GNP—that is, negative growth, or even GNP that is growing at a lower rate than had been expected—can foster civil strife and political instability by stifling popular expectations.

Given the underlying assumption that economically developed countries *tend* to be more politically stable, all other things being equal, a strong argument can be made that energy consumption per capita in these developing countries is both a reflection of the ability of the political system to function and a forecast of things to come, since growth often leads to further growth. Energy consumption per capita is also an indicator of a range of other development activities, such as urbanization, literacy, and improvements in the economic infrastructure. Since these activities are often associated with system stability because of their relationship to increased well-being at the individual level and less generalized discontent, energy consumption per capita is a useful summary indicator of general economic development.

The second major component of the PSSI is the Societal Conflict Index. Unlike the socioeconomic indicators, which probe the underlying causes of and the potential for instability stemming from ethnolinguistic cleavages and economic sources, the constituent variables of the Societal Conflict Index tap political conflict that has already disrupted the system. Such indicators are of potential use in forecasting future instability, since an impressive amount of research on the causes of political violence has supported the thesis that violence leads to further violence. As Rummel, Tanter, and others have noted, domestic political conflict can be typologized into several components.[8] Consequently, the Societal Conflict component of the PSSI was divided into indicators of Public Unrest, Internal Violence, and the Coercion Potential of the society.

Three indicators compose the Public Unrest Index: the

number of (1) demonstrations, (2) riots, and (3) government crises. All three indicators reveal to some degree the extent of public dissatisfaction either with government policies or with the government itself. A demonstration was defined as a peaceful public gathering of at least 100 people for the primary purpose of displaying opposition to government policies or authority. A riot was defined as a demonstration involving the use of force and resulting in material damage or bloodshed. A government crisis was defined as a rapidly developing situation that threatens to bring about the immediate downfall of the government.[9] These riots, demonstrations, and crises may be aimed only at replacing the leadership elites or changing government policy. Therefore, riots or demonstrations may have little direct bearing on the inherent stability of the political system as a whole. Nevertheless, these indicators of public unrest do reflect public dissatisfaction and provide an estimate of the pressure for change in the political system. Because these indicators may not tap the stability of the political system directly, they were only given half the weight of the other two components of the Societal Conflict Index.

The Internal Violence Index is composed of four indicators: the number of (1) armed attacks, (2) assassinations, (3) coups d'etat, and (4) guerrilla warfare incidents.[10] Each of these variables has a much higher potential for disrupting the political system than do the Public Unrest indicators. Armed attacks were defined as acts of violent political conflict carried out by organized groups with the object of weakening or destroying the power exercised by another organized group. Assassination was defined as the politically motivated murder or attempted murder of a high government official or politician. Coups d'état were defined as attempts by officers of the armed forces or police or by members of the ruling elite to overthrow the central government by force or threat of force. Guerrilla warfare incidents were defined as armed activity on the part of bands of citizens or irregular forces aimed at the overthrow of the existing government. Such activity may take the form of sporadic attacks on police posts, villages, government patrols, or military barracks.

The effects of such political violence on the stability of the political system are clear. Such activities are often not based on opposition to a particular government policy. Rather, they may be motivated by opposition to the means by which conflicting values are resolved within a society. They may often be aimed at changing the political system itself. Typically, they are the product of deep-seated grievances that are unlikely to be assuaged by simple policy changes. Accordingly, they are useful indicators of future internal violence.

The third component of the Societal Conflict Index is the society's coercion potential. A political system's ability to function depends, in part, on its ability to punish certain forms of behavior and reinforce others. The sole variable selected as an indicator of this capability—the number of internal security forces per thousand persons in the working-age population—is appropriate for several reasons. Not only is it an indicator of the government's perception of the internal threats it faces (as well as selected external threats as they may interact with domestic threats), but it is also a gross measure of the government's "insecurity." The size of these forces reflects calculations of the number needed to maintain order. Use of another variable—for example, the size of the armed forces per thousand persons—was considered, since these forces also serve internal security functions in many Third World countries. However, this variable was rejected because the size of the armed forces often depends on external considerations (such as the threat of or the existence of a state of belligerency) and because certain segments of the armed forces—the navy and air force—usually do not serve internal security purposes.[11]

The third major component of the PSSI refers to the political system's governmental characteristics, which have collectively been labeled Governmental Processes. Four variables make up this index: (1) constitutional changes per year, (2) legislative effectiveness, (3) political competition, and (4) the number of irregular executive changes.[12]

The number of constitutional changes per year was defined as the number of basic alterations in a country's constitutional structure, the extreme case being the adoption of a new constitution that significantly alters the prerogatives of the various branches of government. Amendments with no significant impact on the political system were not counted. Since a constitution usually defines a society's basic political procedures, frequent significant changes betray fundamental disagreements on the political "rules of the game."

Legislative effectiveness was coded along a four-point scale. If no legislature existed, a 0 (zero) was coded. If legislative activity was essentially of a "rubber stamp" character, if domestic turmoil made the implementation of legislation impossible, or if the executive prevented the legislature from meeting or substantially impeded its functions, then a 1 for "ineffective" legislature was coded. If the executive's power substantially outweighed, but did not completely dominate, that of the legislature, then a 2 for "partially effective" legislature was coded. If the legislature had significant governmental autonomy, including taxation authority and the ability to override an executive veto, then a 3 for "effective" legislature was coded. In countries where the legislature is nonexistent or serves merely as a "rubber stamp," the potential for rapid change is great. Effective legislatures, in contrast, frequently delay decisions pending a full hearing or discussion of proposed new policies and often compromise originally proposed policies. Consequently, decisions often reflect the interests of all concerned more fully. Moreover, the delay in implementing a proposed policy change can provide time for accommodation and adaptation within the political system.

The third component of the Governmental Processes Index is a measure of political competitiveness, derived from a combination of variables that measure the competitiveness of the nominating process, the presence of legislative coalitions, legislative effectiveness, and the degree of party legitimacy.[13] Again, this indicator was not selected to measure governments against some idealized democratic system. Rather, the greater the competition institutionalized by the political system and the more that different interests are legitimately represented, the less likely it is that segments of the society will seek solutions to their grievances outside these forums.

The fourth component of the Governmental Processes Index is the number of irregular executive changes. This indicator was defined as a change in office of the national executive from one leader or ruling group to another that is accomplished outside the conventional legal or customary procedures for transferring formal power. It is frequently accompanied by actual or threatened violence. Although it encompasses coups,[14] it also includes other types of irregular executive changes, such as those that result from purges or internal reshuffling of cabinets. Frequent irregular executive changes are indicative of a political system's fundamental instability and suggest the potential for rapid reversal of governmental policies.

The Socioeconomic, Societal Conflict, and Governmental Processes Indexes are weighted equally in constructing the PSSI. First, all three indexes make different but important contributions to the stability of a political system. Each component is capable of destabilizing a system, yet each could be considered necessary to foster stability. Second, it would be empirically difficult, if not impossible, to separate each component's independent contributions to the system's stability.

APPENDIX B:
Investment Insurance Programs of the Industrial Countries[1]

Summary

Thirteen industrial countries have created programs to insure their investors against the political risks (war, expropriation, and inconvertibility) of investing abroad. Most of the programs will insure only in less developed countries (LDCs) and only those investments that have a developmental effect on the host country's economy.

The United States established the first such scheme in 1948, although the Overseas Private Investment Corporation (OPIC), currently responsible for the program, did not come into being until 1969. The program was relatively little used before 1959, when it was redirected toward LDCs. Growth was rapid in the 1960s. Japan and the Federal Republic of Germany initiated programs in 1956 and 1960, respectively; the other ten did so during the 1960s and early 1970s.

OPIC is by far the largest insurer, followed by Japan's Ministry of International Trade and Industry (MITI) and Germany's Treuarbeit. The United Kingdom's Export Credits Guarantee Department (ECGD) and Canada's Export Development Corporation (EDC), while next in terms of size, are newer and much smaller. All of these programs are broadly similar in their eligibility requirements and general contractual terms, although Japan's and Germany's charge a lower premium rate than the others. OPIC, the only one that has had to pay substantial sums in claims, has the highest premium rate.

The Japanese program, relatively inactive until its reorganization in 1970, is now the fastest growing insurer. OPIC's growth rate, in contrast, leveled off in the early 1970s as the organization began to manage its risks more systematically than had its predecessor agencies. (In this way, OPIC hopes to be able to operate on a self-sustaining basis as well as meet the private participation requirements set by Congress in 1974.) The German program is expanding at a modest rate, while the two most recent of the major programs, the UK's (1972) and Canada's (1969), are growing somewhat more rapidly.

*   *   *

Governments of a number of industrial countries have set up programs to insure their nationals against the political (i.e., noncommercial) risks of investing in foreign countries. Most of the programs are limited to investment in less developed countries, but a few insure worldwide. All programs but those of the British and the French include a requirement that the investment foster economic development in the host country. The investing countries look to their own interests as well, and many of them list "promotion of economic relations" between the investing and host countries as a program objective. Export expansion is doubtless one of the major benefits anticipated by the investing country, but only two programs, the French and the Danish, set this as an explicit requirement.

The U.S. investment insurance program was the first. The Overseas Private Investment Corporation, established by law in 1969, did not begin formal operation until January 1, 1971, but its forerunners in the Agency for International Development and predecessor agencies date back to 1948. The early U.S. program was limited in scope; inconvertibility insurance for equity investment was the only coverage available until 1950, when the guarantee was extended to cover expropriation risks. War risks were added in 1956. At the end of 1958, $400 million in coverage had been issued, $321 million of which involved investment in Western Eurpoe. An increasing number of investors utilized the program after it was redirected toward LDCs in 1959. When OPIC began operations in 1971, $8.4 billion in insurance policies[2] had been isued under AID's Special Risk Investment Guaranty Program and its predecessors.

The Japanese program was established in 1956, but the total investment insured through April 1970, when there were major changes in the program, was only $68.6 million. The West German program, established in 1960, was the third. By 1971, Treuarbeit had insured $72.4 million of German direct investment in LDCs.

Following the example of the U.S., Japan, and Germany, ten other industrial countries (Australia, Belgium, Canada, Denmark, France, the Netherlands, Norway, Sweden, Switzerland, and the United Kingdom) initiated investment insurance programs in the 1960s and early 1970s.

Major Features of Selected Insurance Programs

The four programs that are most comparable to the U.S. insurance scheme by virtue of their size and significance are those of Canada, the Federal Republic of Germany, Japan, and the United Kingdom. A review of Tables 1 and 2, below, indicates broad areas of similarity among the various programs with respect to eligible countries and investors, developmental requirements, risks covered, and general contractual terms.

Certain exceptions should be noted. In the area of country eligibility, Germany's Treuarbeit, as a rule, insures investments only in countries where a bilateral investment protection agreement is in force. Exceptions are made in cases where Treuarbeit determines that a nation's local laws concerning investment would afford the investor a comparable level of protection.

OPIC varies from the norm in that it will insure an investment for a maximum duration of 20 years; the limit for most of the other countries' programs is 15 years. In addition, OPIC, together with the United Kingdom's ECGD, offers the greatest opportunity for coverage of reinvested earnings and for increases in the amount of investment covered by a given contract (Table 2).

On the restrictive side, OPIC, unlike its counterparts in other nations, does not insure investment when the foreign enterprise is a public entity.

The most notable exception to the overall similarity in contractual terms is found in the area of combined premium rates

TABLE 1: ELIGIBILITY REQUIREMENTS

	Canada (EDC)	Fed. Rep. of Germany (Treuarbeit)	Japan (MITI)	United Kingdom (ECGD)	United States (OPIC)
Geographic Coverage					
LDCs only		x^1			X
Worldwide			x^2	x^2	
Other	x^3				
Types of Investment					
Equity	X	X	X	X	X
Loans	X	X	X	X	X
Licenses and Royalties	X	X		X	X
Real Estate, Portfolios, Long-Term Loans for Resource Supply			X		
Investor Eligibility Requirements					
National Ownership	50%				Majority
National Domicile/ Incorporation		Domicile or 50% German-owned	Incorporated under Japanese law	British-owned or Domiciled in UK	
Insure only national share in Consortium	X	X			X
Foreign Enterprise Eligibility Requirements					
New, Direct Investment	X	X	X	X	X
Foster Development	X	X	X		X
Private Entity					X

[1] Must be country with which FRG has concluded investment protection agreement, or whose local laws are found to offer comparable protection of investment.

[2] Most investment under cover is in LDCs.

[3] LDCs and Eastern Europe; 12.6% of insured investment is in Europe.

collected by the insurers (Table 2). The German and Japanese programs' rates are near the .5 percent level; those of Canada and the United Kingdom, while somewhat higher, do not exceed 1 percent. OPIC charges between 1.3 and 2.1 percent and has recently included provisions in its contracts whereby rates may be increased by as much as 50 percent during the first 10 years of a contract. It is not clear whether the higher OPIC premium rates are a disincentive to prospective users of the program, although OPIC officials report some assertions by firms to this effect. However,

TABLE 2: CONTRACTUAL TERMS

	Canada	Fed. Rep. of Germany	Japan	United Kingdom	United States
Percentage Covered					
Initial Investment	100	100	100	100	90
Reinvested Earnings	50	50		100	90
Remitted Earnings	150	8[1]	100	100	90
Annual Premiums (Percentage)					
War	0.3				0.6-1
Expropriation	0.3				0.4-0.8
Inconvertibility	0.3				0.3
Total	0.9	0.5	0.55	1.0	1.3-2.1
Total and Credit Risks			0.7		
Standby				0.5	0.25[2]
Other Provisions					
Percentage Loss Payable	85	95	90	90	50-100
Maximum Duration (years)	15	15	15	15	20
Possibility for Increase in Coverage (percent)	none	150	none	200	200
Types of Risk					
War, Revolution, Insurrection	X	X	X	X	X
Expropriation, Nationalization, Confiscation	X	X	X	X	X
Inconvertibility	X	X	X	X	X

[1]Annually for maximum of three years.

[2]On standby amount.

OPIC's rates are much lower than those of commercial insurers, and its contract terms are generally broader.

OPIC has set comparatively high premium rates for several reasons—to meet its claims requirements, particularly with regard to a number of inherently high-risk minerals projects insured prior to 1971; to adhere to its mandate to be self-sustaining; and to attract private-sector participation in issuing political risk insurance.[3]

None of the other programs has had to pay as substantial claims as OPIC relative to total insurance issued (Table 3). For the German program, claims may have been reduced by its numerous bilateral agreements with LDCs on legal safeguards for direct investment. Claims under the Japanese program have been very low in comparison with its present size, but the sharp increases in coverage since 1970, and particularly in 1974 and 1975, may bring more claims in the future.

TABLE 3: PROGRAM ACTIVITY--GLOBAL CEILING,
CLAIMS, AMOUNT UNDER COVER
(As of December 1975)

Country Agency	Global Ceiling	Claims	Total Investment Under Cover	Percentage Direct Investment in LDCs Insured by Programs
Canada (EDC)	$250 million	None	$69.5 million	7.4
Fed. Rep. of Germany (Treuarbeit)	Fixed by annual budget	6 claims paid $850,000	$588 million	12.2
Japan (MITI)	Annual ceiling $1,000 million	12 claims paid $1,100,000	$1,900 million	33.3
UK (ECGD)	$500 million	None	$71.3 million	3.5
US (OPIC)	$7,500 million	45 claims paid $98,900,000	$4,200 million	10.9

A sudden deluge of claims payments might result in higher premium rates for other programs. On the other hand, all programs are government-sponsored, and the governments are liable, ultimately, for the payment of claims. Under the German program, claims are paid by appropriations from the treasury, and the fees collected are used only to defray operating expenses. Whether this is the intent of other governments as well is not yet apparent. It is clear, however, that OPIC's large reserves afford better protection against the need for treasury funds to meet claims payments than do the smaller reserves of the other programs.

Moreover, the appropriateness of a government-sponsored political risk insurance program has not been questioned in the other countries as it has been in the United States. Therefore, these programs are less concerned than is OPIC about carrying on a self-sustaining operation, and they do not have to contend with the issue of privatization.

Current Status of the Major Programs

The U.S., Japanese, and German programs are by far the largest, with investment under cover at the end of 1975 of $4.2 billion, $1.9

billion, and $588 million, respectively. The UK program, although it was only established in 1972, is next, with $71.3 million of investment under cover, closely followed by the Canadian program with $69.5 million under cover (Figure 1).

The U.S. Program

The early 1970s witnessed a leveling off in the underwriting of insurance. OPIC coverage continued to grow, but not as rapidly as did U.S. direct investment in LDCs during the same period (Table 4).[4] A possible explanation is that the size of U.S. firms and the geographic diversity of their foreign investments have allowed many of them to self-insure, thereby forgoing the use of government-sponsored insurance with its relatively high premiums, inflexibility, and red tape.

Two other factors, one sectoral and the other regional, may also have contributed to the slowing down of insurance activities. Sectorally, there has been a significant decrease in investment in the metal mining field. Twenty-five percent of the insurance written by OPIC's predecessor agencies involved metal-mining investment. OPIC has issued only 3 percent of its overall coverage in this sector.

Regionally, there is the reluctance of U.S. investors to undertake new projects in Latin America (excepting Brazil and the Caribbean area), a reluctance caused in large part by increased economic nationalism in certain countries of the region, and by the implementation of restrictive investment codes in others. The decrease in 1974 in the total amount of U.S. investment under cover (Figure 1) coincides with the takeover of a number of OPIC-insured investments in Latin American countries. Once an area of heavy insurance activity, Latin America has seen its share in OPIC's overall commitments drop from 56.1 percent in 1973 to 40.1 percent in 1975 (Table 5). Policies in the region accounted for only 27 percent of the coverage provided by OPIC in FY 1976.

Since 1971, OPIC management has been applying risk-management techniques not emphasized by its predecessor agencies in order to continue operation on a self-sustaining basis, as well as to fulfill the privatization goals mandated by Congress in a series of 1974 amendments to the Foreign Assistance Act of 1961.

178

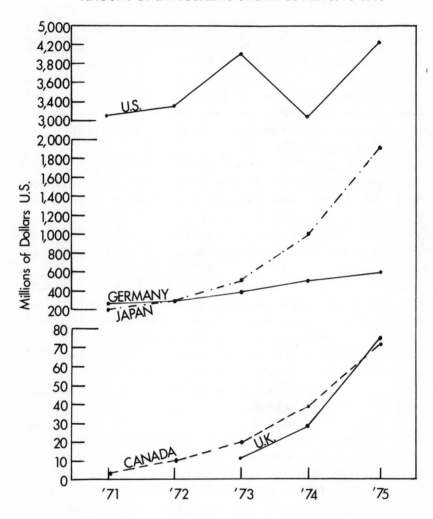

Figure 1
SELECTED COUNTRIES
AMOUNT OF INVESTMENT UNDER COVER 1971–1975

TABLE 4: INSURED INVESTMENT AS A PERCENTAGE OF
SUM OF INVESTMENT FLOWS TO LDCs
(US$ millions)

	1971	1972	1973	1974	1975
Canada					
A. Amount of Investment Under Cover	3	7	23	43	69.5
B. Cumulative Investment Flow to LDCs	140.2	316.2	441.2	634.2	934.2
C. A as Percentage of B	2.17%	2.2%	5.2%	6.8%	7.4%
Fed. Rep. of Germany					
A. Amount of Investment Under Cover	261	302	406	491	588
B. Cumulative Investment Flow to LDCs	1,898.0	2,499.2	3,285.8	3,987.1	4,803.0
C. A as Percentage of B	13.8%	12.1%	12.4%	12.3%	12.2%
Japan					
A. Amount of Investment Under Cover	219	308	467	1,075	1,900
B. Cumulative Investment Flow to LDCs	1,419.7	1,623.7	2,924.8	4,500[1]	5,700[1]
C. A as Percentage of B	15.4%	19.0%	16.0%	23.9%	33.3%
United Kingdom					
A. Amount of Investment Under Cover			13	30	71.3
B. Cumulative Investment Flow to LDCs			698.8	1,393.5	2,060
C. A as Percentage of B			1.9%	2.2%	3.5%
United States					
A. Amount of Investment Under Cover	3,141	3,364	3,739	2,985	4,200
B. Cumulative Investment Flow to LDCs	22,815	24,791	27,678	31,456	38,533
C. A as Percentage of B	13.8%	13.6%	13.5%	9.5%	10.9%

[1]Approximate figure.

Other Major Programs

The Japanese program expanded significantly in the early 1970's, a development coincident with increased Japanese interest in direct investment in LDCs as a means of reducing disproportionate balance of payments surpluses and of ensuring access to raw material supplies. From the inception of the program in 1956 through 1970, only $68.8 million of Japanese investment abroad was covered by insurance. In May 1970, however, the program was reorganized to make it more responsive to the needs of the Japanese investor. The two earlier schemes—Overseas Invest-

TABLE 5: GEOGRAPHIC DISTRIBUTION OF INSURANCE COVERAGE,
DECEMBER 1975
(in percentages)

Country Agency	Africa	Asia	Europe	Latin America	Middle East	Oceania
Canada (EDC)	7.9	27.8	12.6	27.4	24.1	
Fed. Rep. of Germany (Treuarbeit)	35.2	15.2	7.9	26.1	9.8	
Japan (MITI)	2.1	58	1	26.1	5.1	2.4
UK (ECGD)	23.6	4.6	0.4	55.8	15.6	
US (OPIC)	10.9	35.3	0.7	40.1	12.8	

ment Principal Insurance (1956), which protected capital against expropriation and war risks, and Overseas Investment Profit Insurance (1957), which covered profits against nonconvertibility risks—were merged into a single program administered by the Ministry of International Trade and Industry.

Under the old scheme, only equity investment was insurable; the amended program covers loans and advances as well. The compensation rate was raised from 75 percent under the old program to 90 percent under the new, and the requirements for compensation were relaxed so that liquidation of the investment is no longer a prerequisite for payment. It is sufficient to demonstrate that losses incurred are large enough to make continued operation of the investment project impossible.

Finally, annual premium rates were gradually lowered during the 1960s to a rate of .499 percent in 1970. (The current rate is .55 percent.)

Following the reorganization, the program grew rapidly, and by March 1972, the amount of investment under cover had risen to $267.8 million. By December 1975, the total amount under cover was $1.9 billion, with 85 percent of the 1972-75 coverage issued in 1974 and 1975.

Comparable data concerning the early years of the German program are not available, but the data that can be obtained (number and size of approved insurance applications) indicate that the German program has grown at a steady, although not spectacular rate, with 1965 and 1974 being its two most active years. According to an OECD study, program improvements were made in 1963 and 1964, which may have contributed in part to increased Treuarbeit activity in 1965.

The FRG has been more active than most other industrial nations in concluding comprehensive bilateral agreements that are intended to provide maximum legal safeguards for the protection of German direct investment in LDCs. Forty-seven such agreements are currently in force. It is possible that the German program would be more heavily used were it not for the security already provided the German investor by these agreements.

The two most recent programs, the UK's ECGD (July 1972) and Canada's EDC (October 1969), have been growing steadily since their inception, but it is too soon to determine any pattern in their growth rates. Having had the three major programs as models, the ECGD and EDC may experience less severe "growing pains" than did the U.S., Japanese, and German programs, each of which underwent varying degrees of modification before they were able to prove useful to a significant number of investors.

Overall, one measure of the significance of these programs to prospective investors is the relationship between the amount of total investment under cover for each program and the flow of direct investment to LDCs from the inception of that program (Table 5).

By this criterion, Japan leads with one-third of Japanese investment in LDCs insured by MITI, a figure that appears to be on the increase. The FRG and the United States have insured 12.2 percent and 10.9 percent,[5] respectively, of their countries' total investment in LDCs, a figure that, for both, has dropped slightly since 1971. Canada's percentage is now 7.4 percent, and that of the United Kingdom, 3.5 percent.

Other Countries' Programs

Among the eight remaining programs, Switzerland's is the largest, with $50.1 million in investment under cover, followed by

Australia ($41.4 million), France ($28.1 million), the Netherlands ($23.02 million), Denmark ($17.4 million), and Belgium ($7.5 million). The Swedish program, limited to 11 African countries, has such stringent eligibility requirements that it has yet to issue any insurance.

France, although a major foreign investor, has been relatively inactive in the field of investment insurance. Program responsibilities are divided among three agencies, each with its own clientele. For these agencies, the underwriting of investment insurance has been a residual function, second in importance to schemes more directly linked to the promotion of French exports.

The annex provides a list of the eight above-mentioned programs and a summary of their operations.

ANNEX: INVESTMENT INSURANCE PROGRAMS

Country Agency	Eligible Countries	Types of Risks Insured 1. War 2. Expropriation 3. Inconvertibility 4. Other	Types of Investment Insured 1. Equity 2. Loans 3. Licenses 4. Other
Australia Export Finance and Insurance Corporation (EFIC) 1966	Worldwide	1,2,3	1,2,3
Belgium Office National dueDucroire(OND) 1971	Worldwide	1,2,3,4 (catastrophe)	1,2
Denmark Danish International Development Agency (DANIDA) 1966	LDCs	1,2,3	1,2,3
France Compagnie Francaise d'Assurance pour le Commerce Extérieur (COFACE) 1971	Worldwide	1,2,3,4 (nonpayment)	1,2,3
Banque Francaise du Commerce Exterieur (BFCE)	14 LDCs	1,2,3	1
Caisse Centrale de Cooperation Eco- nomique (CCCE) 1971	12 African LDCs	1,2,3	1
Netherlands Netherlands Credit Insurance Company (NCM) 1969	LDCs	1,2,3	1,2,3
Norway Guarantee Institute (GI) 1964	LDCs	1,2,3,4 (discrimi- natory taxation)	1,2,3
Sweden Swedish Export Credits Guarantee Board (EKN) 1968	11 LDCs	1,2,3	1,2,4 (technology)
Switzerland Office for Guaran- teeing Investment Risk (GIRG) 1970	LDCs	1,2,3,4 (nonpayment)	1,2,4 (technology)

INVESTMENT INSURANCE PROGRAMS (2)

Country Agency	Eligibility Requirements for Investors 1. Must be in national interest 2. May be public or private entity 3. Only national's share in multi- national consortium insurable 4. Other	Eligibility Requirements for Foreign Enterprises 1. Must be new, direct investment 2. Must foster economic develop- ment in host country 3. May be public or private entity
Australia EFIC	1,2,3	1,2,3
Belgium OND	4 (must be enterprise active in Belgian economic community)	1,2,3
Denmark DANIDA	3,4 (must be linked to Danish exports)	1,2,3
France COFACE BFCE CCCE	4 (must be linked to French exports) 4 (must develop French economy) 4 (must develop French economy)	3 1 1
Netherlands NCM	4 (must be private, Dutch-owned firm or established in Netherlands)	1,2,3
Norway GI	4 (must be private, Norwegian- owned firm)	2,3
Sweden EKN	1	1,2,3
Switzerland GIRG	4 (must be Swiss-owned or domiciled in Switzerland)	2,3

INVESTMENT INSURANCE PROGRAMS (3)

Country Agency	Coverages 1. Initial Investment 2. Reinvested Earnings 3. Remitted Earnings	Loss Payable	Maximum Duration	Possibility for Increase in Amount Covered
Australia EFIC	1 (100%) 2 (100%) 3 (100%)	90%	15 years	None
Belgium OND	1 (100%) 2 (100%) 3 (100%)	90%	15 years	Up to 150%
Denmark DANIDA	1 (100%) 2 - 3 (24%)	90%	15 years	Up to amount of reinvested earnings
France COFACE	Up to 15% of export contract's value or exports of 5 years to come	90%	15 years	None
BFCE	1 (100%) 2 (50%) 3 -	90%	15 years	None
CCCE	1 (100%) 2 (50%) 3 -	90%	15 years	None
Netherlands NCM	1 (100%) 2 (50%) 3 (8% per annum)	90%	20 years	Up to 150%
Norway GI	1 (100%) 2 (100%) 3 (24%)	60-90%	20 years	None
Sweden EKN	1 (100%) 2 - 3 (up to 24%)	90%	15 years	None
Switzerland GIRG	1 (100%) 2 - 3 (up to 24%)	70%	15 years	Up to 200%

12186

INVESTMENT INSURANCE PROGRAMS (4)

Country Agency	Annual Premium 1. War 2. Expropriation 3. Inconvertibility	Global Ceiling	Total Investment Under Cover as of December 1975
Australia EFIC	1. (.24-.30%) 2. (.32-.40%) 3. (.24-.30%) Total (.80-100%)	$250 million	$41.4 million
Belgium OND	1. (.25%) 2. (.25%) 3. (.25%) Total (.75%)	None	$7.5 million
Denmark DANIDA	total (.5%)	$81 million	$17.4 million
France COFACE BFCE CCCE	total (.8%) total (.8%) total (.8%)	None None None	$20.9 million $ 1.5 million $ 5.7 million
Netherlands NCM	total (.8%)	Fixed annual ceiling - $8.3 million (1972)	$23.02 million
Norway GI	total (.5-.7%)	$92 million for invest. insurance and export credit	$21.9 million
Sweden EKN	total (.7%)	$77 million	None
Switzerland GIRG	total (1.25%) total + profits (4% of expected amt.)	$180 million	$50.1 million

INVESTMENT INSURANCE PROGRAMS (5)

Country Agency	Geographic Distribution as of December 1975		Claims as of December 1975	Percentage of Direct Foreign Investment in LDCs Insured by Program as of December 1975
Australia EFIC	Asia	(90%)	None	6.3
	Latin America	(1.3%)		
	Japan & So. Africa	(4.6%)		
	Middle East	(1.2%)		
	Oceania	(1.6%)		
Belgium OND	Africa	(38.3%)	None	3.3
	Asia	(18.3%)		
	Latin America	(7.2%)		
	Europe	(36%)		
Denmark DANIDA	Not available		None	18.3
France COFACE	Africa	(7.9%)	None	1.3
	Asia	(33.9%)		
	Latin America	(17.2%)		
	Middle East	(3.4%)		
	Europe	(37.4%)		
BFCE	Brazil	(54.3%)	None	1.3
	Iran	(27.4%)		
	Tunisia	(18.4%)		
CCCE	Africa	(100%)	None	1.3
Netherlands NCM	Africa	(16.7%)	None	1.9
	Asia	(74.5%)		
	Latin America	(8.6%)		
Norway GI	Africa	(5.5%)	None	21.4
	Asia	(4.6%)		
	Latin America	(89.8%)		
Sweden EKN	None		None	None
Switzerland GIRG	Africa	(47.8%)	None	9
	Asia	(0.9%)		
	Latin America	(45.3%)		
	Middle East	(5.5%)		
	Europe	(0.4%)		

Notes

Preface

1. David K. Eiteman, "American Portfolio Investor Discounting of Political and Social Risks in Cuban Securities," *The Quarterly Review of Economics and Business*, May 1962, pp. 89-98.

Introduction

1. However, some LDCs may adopt a more pragmatic approach toward foreign investment because they need its benefits.

2. Hearings were conducted in 1973 and 1974 by the House Subcommittee on Foreign Economic Policy and in 1973 by the Senate Subcommittee on the Multinational Corporation.

3. Hearings were conducted in 1977 and 1978 by the Subcommittee on International Economic Policy and Trade of the Committee on International Relations, in addition to the full committee of the House, and in 1977 by the Subcommittee on Foreign Assistance of the Senate Committee on Foreign Relations.

4. Dan Haendel, Gerald T. West, and Robert G. Meadow, *Overseas Investment and Political Risk* (Philadelphia: Foreign Policy Research Institute, 1975). The term *political risk* conforms to this definition unless the context indicates that reference is to (1) OPIC's insurable risks (war, expropriation, and inconvertibility of assets) or (2) another agency's or author's use of the term. When confusion may arise over the technical definition of *political risk*, as opposed to the above definition, the term *political risk* has been set off in quotation marks to denote the latter meaning.

Chapter 1

1. Sanford Rose, "Why the Multinational Tide is Ebbing," *Fortune*, August 1977, pp. 111-120.

2. U.S., Congress, Senate, Committee on Foreign Relations, Subcommittee on Foreign Assistance, *Hearings on OPIC Authorization*, 95th Cong., 1st sess., July 27, 29 and August 4, 1977 (Washington, D.C.: Government Printing Office, 1977), pp. 144, 148.

3. The analysis that follows is based primarily on Herbert Mayer, "Dow Picks up the Pieces in Chile," *Fortune*, April 1974.

4. Ibid., p. 142.

5. Ibid., p. 152.

6. Ibid.

7. Philip R. Cateora, "The Multinational Enterprise and Nationalism," *MSU Business Topics*, Spring 1971, p. 49.

8. Seymour J. Rubin, "Transnational Corporations: Supervision, Regulation, or What?" *The International Trade Law Journal*, Spring 1975, p. 12.

9. Senate, *Hearings on OPIC Authorization*, p. 11.

10. J. Frederick Truitt, "Expropriation of Foreign Investment: Summary of the Post World War II Experience of American and British Investors in the Less Developed Countries," *Journal of International Business Studies*, Fall 1970, p. 28.

11. Ibid.

12. Ibid., p. 34.

13. Franklin Root, "The Expropriation Experience of American Companies: What Happened to 38 Companies," *Business Horizons*, April 1968, p. 69.

14. Ibid., p. 74.

15. See, for example, Bernard A. Lietaer, "Managing Risks in Foreign Exchange," *Harvard Business Review*, March-April 1970.

16. Theodore H. Moran, "Transnational Strategies of Protection and Defense by Multinational Corporations: Spreading the Risk and Raising the Cost for Nationalization in Natural Resources," *International Organization*, Spring 1973, p. 277.

17. Ibid., p. 279.

18. Theodore H. Moran, "New Deal or Raw Deal in Raw Materials," *Foreign Policy*, Winter 1971-1972, pp. 123-124.

19. Ibid., pp. 125-126.

20. Senate, *Hearings on OPIC Authorization*, pp. 12-13.

21. U.S., Congress, House, Committee on International Relations, Subcommittee on International Economic Policy and Trade, *Corporate*

Business Practices and United States Foreign Policy, 95th Cong., 1st sess., September 7, 1977, pp. 10-11.

22. Ibid., p. 58 (Testimony of Paul H. Boeker, deputy assistant secretary of state for economic and business affairs).

23. Ibid., p. 4.

24. Ibid., pp. 61-62.

25. Ibid., pp. 60-61.

26. Senate, *Hearings on OPIC Authorization*, p. 8.

27. Irving S. Friedman, *The Emerging Role of Private Banks in the Developing World* (New York: Citicorp, 1977).

28. Richard J. Barnet and Ronald E. Müller, *Global Reach* (New York: Simon and Schuster, 1974).

29. Cateora, "The Multinational Enterprise and Nationalism," p. 52.

30. U.S. Congress, Senate, Committee on Foreign Relations, Subcommittee on Multinational Corporations, *Hearing on the International Telephone and Telegraph Co. and Chile*, 93rd Cong., 1st sess., 1973. See also Anthony Sampson, *The Sovereign State of ITT* (New York: Stein and Day, 1973).

31. Ronald Müller, "Poverty Is the Product," *Foreign Policy*, Winter 1973-1974. See also Barnet and Müller, *Global Reach*.

32. Obie G. Whichard, "U.S. Direct Investment Abroad in 1976," *Survey of Current Business*, August 1977.

33. Senate, *Hearings on OPIC Authorization*, p. 14.

34. C. Fred Bergsten, "Coming Investment Wars?" *Foreign Affairs*, October 1974, p. 146.

35. C. Fred Bergsten, "The Threat from the Third World," *Foreign Policy*, Summer 1973, pp. 167-168.

Chapter 2

1. OPIC is authorized to perform several functions other than providing insurance. It operates a finance program and a productive credit guaranty program. It also plays a role in the settlement of investment disputes.

2. U.S., Congress, Senate, Committee on Foreign Relations, *The Investment Insurance Program Managed by the Overseas Private Investment Corporation*, a report by the comptroller general of the United States (Washington, D.C.: Government Printing Office, July 26, 1977).

3. U.S., Congress, Senate, Committee on Foreign Relations, Subcommittee on Multinational Corporations, *Management of Investment Insurance, Loan Guarantees, and Claim Payments by the Overseas Private Investment Corporation*, a report by the comptroller general of the

United States (Washington, D.C.: Government Printing Office, 1973), p. 14.

4. This restriction affects the following states: Argentina, Barbados, Brazil, Brunei, Cyprus, French Guiana, French Polynesia, Gabon, Greece, Guadeloupe, Iran, Israel, Jamaica, Malta, Martinique, Netherlands Antilles, New Caledonia, Oman, Panama, Portugal, Romania, Saudi Arabia, Singapore, Surinam, Trinidad and Tobago, Uruguay, Venezuela, and Yugoslavia.

5. OPIC Release RJ/393, September 26, 1977.

6. See Appendix B.

7. Keith Wheelock, "What Is the Direction of U.S. Political Risk Insurance?" *Columbia Journal of World Business*, Summer 1973, p. 66.

8. U.S., Library of Congress, Congressional Research Service, Foreign Affairs Division, *The Overseas Private Investment Corporation: A Critical Analysis* (Washington, D.C.: Government Printing Office, 1973), p. 64.

9. U.S., Congress, Senate, Committee on Foreign Relations, *Report of the Committee on Foreign Relations on the Overseas Private Investment Corporation Amendment Act* (S. 2957) (Washington, D.C.: Government Printing Office, February 5, 1974), pp. 16-17.

10. Ibid., p. 20.

11. The AFL-CIO noted that U.S. taxpayers might ultimately have to compensate MNEs for losses incurred in foreign countries. This, the AFL-CIO argued, would mean that workers whose jobs were exported in "runaway" industries would pay double—once for lost employment and again through Treasury repayments. See the AFL-CIO legislative report, *Labor Looks at the 93rd Congress* (Washington, D.C.: AFL-CIO Department of Legislation, publication 77p, February 1975), p. 32. See also the testimony of Dr. Rudolph Oswald, director of research, AFL-CIO, before the House Committee on International Relations on H.R. 9179, January 27, 1978.

12. U.S., Congress, House, Committee on Foreign Affairs, Subcommittee on Foreign Economic Policy, *The Overseas Private Investment Corporation*, 93rd Cong., 1st sess. (Washington, D.C.: Government Printing Office, October 21, 1973), p. 36.

13. OPIC Release Ts/262, February 1974, p. 8.

14. Senate, *Report on the Amendment Act*, p. 26.

15. Ibid., p. 32.

16. In the United States, one can now purchase flood or earthquake insurance only as part of an extended property coverage on a standard fire or property insurance policy.

17. U.S., Congress, House, Committee on Foreign Affairs, Subcom-

mittee on Foreign Economic Policy, *The Possibilities of Transferring OPIC Programs to the Private Sector,* report to the Congress by the Overseas Private Investment Corporation, March 20, 1974 (Washington, D.C.: Government Printing Office, 1974), p. 61.

18. Section 240A[b] of the Foreign Assistance Act of 1961, as amended.
19. House, *Transferring OPIC,* p. 63.
20. Ibid., pp. 61-62.
21. *The Overseas Private Investment Corporation,* pp. 37-38.
22. P.L. 93-390, Section 2(2)(B)(4).
23. Senate, *Management of Investment Insurance, Loan Guarantees, and Claim Payments by the Overseas Private Investment Corporation,* p. 22.
24. U.S., Congress, House, Committee on Foreign Affairs, Subcommittee on Foreign Economic Policy, *The Overseas Private Investment Corporation* (Washington, D.C.: Government Printing Office, 1974), p. 64.
25. Ibid., p. 65.
26. Ibid.
27. See *Topics* (Washington, D.C.), September 1974, p. 3. Published by OPIC.
28. Ibid., March/April 1977.
29. Overseas Private Investment Corporation, *1977 Annual Report* (Washington, D.C.: Government Printing Office, 1978).
30. The House Subcommittee on International Economic Policy and Trade held hearings on June 21, 23, July 19, 20, 21, and September 8. Two markup sessions were held on September 12 and 16 on H.R. 7854 and H.R. 3603.
31. The Senate Subcommittee on Foreign Assistance held hearings on July 27, 29, and August 4, 1977. Markup on the bill was on October 11, 1977.
32. U.S., Congress, Senate, Committee on Foreign Relations, *OPIC Amendments Act of 1977* (Washington, D.C.: Government Printing Office, 1977); and U.S., Congress, House, Committee on International Relations, *OPIC Amendments Act of 1977* (Washington, D.C.: Government Printing Office, 1977).
33. House, *OPIC Amendments Act of 1977,* p. 13. See also U.S., Congress, House, Committee on International Trade, Subcommittee on International Economic Policy and Trade, *Hearings and Markup, Extension and Revision of Overseas Private Investment Corporation Programs,* 95th Cong., 1st sess. (Washington, D.C.: Government Printing Office, 1977).
34. House, *Hearings and Markup,* p. 10.

35. Senate, *OPIC Amendments Act of 1977*, p. 15.
36. Senate, *Investment Insurance Program*, p. 8.
37. OPIC, *1977 Annual Report*, p. 46.
38. Senate, *Hearings on OPIC Authorization*, p. 77.
39. Ibid., p. 132.

Chapter 3

1. Fred Greene, "The Management of Political Risk," *Bests Review*, July 1974.
2. Bruce Lloyd, "The Identification and Assessment of Political Risk," *Moorgate and Wall Street*, Spring 1975, p. 56.
3. Ibid.
4. Robert T. Green, *Political Instability as a Determinant of U.S. Foreign Investment* (Austin, Texas: Bureau of Business Research Studies in Marketing, 1972), p. 4.
5. Franklin R. Root, "Analyzing Political Risks in International Business," in *Multinational Enterprise in Transition: Selected Readings and Essays*, ed. A. Kapoor and Phillip Grub (Detroit: Darwin Press, 1972), p. 357.
6. Franklin R. Root, "U.S. Business Abroad and the Political Risks," *MSU Business Topics*, Winter 1968, p. 75.
7. Franklin R. Root, "The Management by LDC Governments of the Political Risk Trade-off in Direct Foreign Investment" (Paper presented at the International Studies Association meeting, Toronto, Canada, February 1976).
8. Root, "U.S. Business," p. 78.
9. See Stefan H. Robock, "Political Risk: Identification and Assessment," *Columbia Journal of World Business*, July-August 1971; idem, "Assessing and Forecasting Political Risk" (Abstract paper for the Research Conference on the Multinational Corporation in the Global Political System, Philadelphia, April 22-23, 1971).
10. Robock, "Political Risk," p. 16.
11. Ibid., pp. 18-19.
12. Robert T. Green, "Political Structures as a Predictor of Radical Political Change," *Columbia Journal of World Business*, Spring 1974 p. 29. Green defines radical political change as "ascendancy to power of a person or group holding a different political philosophy than the person or group it replaced."
13. Robock, "Political Risk," p. 7.
14. Root, "U.S. Business," p. 73.
15. Greene, "Management of Political Risk."
16. Chester William, Jr., and Richard Heins, *Risk Management and*

Insurance (New York: McGraw-Hill, 1964), pp. 4-7.

17. Irving Pfeffer, *Insurance and Economic Theory* (Homewood, Ill.: R. D. Irwin, 1956), p. 42.

18. Allan Willett, *The Economic Theory of Risk and Insurance* (Philadelphia: University of Pennsylvania Press, 1951), p. 6.

19. Ibid., p. 7.

20. Ibid., p. 8.

21. See Yair Aharoni, *The Foreign Investment Decision Process* (Boston: Harvard University, 1966).

22. R. Duncan Luce and Howard Raiffa, *Games and Decisions* (New York: John Wiley and Sons, 1957).

Chapter 4

1. See Bruce M. Russett, *Trends in World Politics* (New York: Macmillan, 1965); Arthur Banks, *Cross-Polity Time-Series Data* (Cambridge, Mass.: MIT Press, 1971); Ivo K. and Rosalind D. Feierabend, "Aggressive Behavior within Polities, 1948-1962: A Cross-National Study," *Journal of Conflict Resolution*, Fall 1966.

2. Robert T. Green and Christopher M. Korth, "Evaluating Political Instability for Foreign Investment Decisions" (Unpublished paper, February 1972).

3. For example, when the Chilean government allegedly persuaded Kennecott Copper to make sizable new investments just before Allende's election.

4. Franklin R. Root, "The Expropriation Experience of American Companies," *Business Horizons*, April 1966.

5. Robert Stobaugh, Jr., "How to Analyze Foreign Investment Climates," *Harvard Business Review*, September-October 1969, pp. 101-102.

6. *New York Times*, September 29, 1974, p. 14.

7. Hans H. Hartleben, "Country Exposure Guidelines," *The Journal of Commercial Bank Lending*, August 1972, p. 9.

8. "A Primer on Country Risk," *Argus Capital Market Report*, June 4, 1975.

9. Ibid.

10. Antoine Van Agtmael, "How Business Has Dealt with Political Risk" (Paper presented at the Conference on Measurement of Political Risk and Foreign Investment Strategy, sponsored by the Foreign Policy Research Institute, Philadelphia, May 9-10, 1975). This paper deals in part with different ways of viewing the profitability and nature of an investment.

11. The operations and financial subindexes of the BERI index appear to be of some use to an investor interested in a comparative evaluation of these risks.

12. F. T. Haner, "Business Environmental Risk Index" (Paper presented to the American Risk and Insurance Association, August 1974), p. 3.

13. Antoine Van Agtmael, "Evaluating the Risks of Lending to Developing Countries," *Euromoney*, April 1976.

14. BI 1972 and BERI 1974 (2d quarter) had rho = 0.894, Student's t = 11.96, $P < 0.0001$, and N = 38.

15. For details on the data and application of the model, see Harald Knudsen, "Explaining the National Propensity to Expropriate: An Ecological Approach," *Journal of International Business Studies*, Spring 1974.

16. This idealized example is not intended to be a complete or realistic illustration of the process by which a corporation evaluates the risks and rewards of a proposed investment. For an analysis of how foreign investment decisions are often made, see Yair Aharoni, *The Foreign Investment Decision Process* (Cambridge, Mass.: Harvard University Press, 1966).

17. Stobaugh, "How to Analyze Foreign Investment Climates."

18. Dan Haendel, Gerald T. West, and Robert G. Meadow, *Overseas Investment and Political Risk* (Philadelphia: Foreign Policy Research Institute, 1975).

19. Most of the work on the PSSI was done by Robert G. Meadow and Gerald T. West.

20. Adam Przeworski and Henry Teune, *The Logic of Comparative Social Inquiry* (New York: John Wiley and Sons, 1970), Chapter 5.

21. The methods employed to construct the PSSI could, of course, be extended to construct a measure that would encompass these countries. However, that would involve a considerable number of complex trade-offs in accuracy.

22. See Table 4.2, for example, for the relative contributions of these components to the PSSI scores for Costa Rica and Romania.

23. R. J. Rummel and David A. Heenan, "How to Analyze Political Risk" (Paper, 1977). This paper has been published under the title "How Multinationals Analyze Political Risk," *Harvard Business Review*, January-February 1978, pp. 67-76.

24. "Investment Appeal Rating of 53 Nations," *The Japan Economic Journal*, August 16, 1977.

25. As for assessment standards for the market-oriented type, the following were taken into account: (1) political environment (political stability; weight: 10 percent); (2) labor factors (such as wage levels and

productivity; weight: 10 percent); (3) industrial infrastructure (such as number of cars; weight: 10 percent); (4) market environment (such as per capita GNP; weight: 30 percent); (5) foreign investment conditions (such as controls on investments; weight: 20 percent); (6) external relations (such as foreign currency reserves; weight: 10 percent); (7) relations with Japan (such as trade balance; weight: 10 percent). These were then graded on a weighted average according to individual factors, such as wage levels, and the overall points (maximum 100 points) were derived based on the weighted average of the medium classification.

As for assessment standards for the resource and processing type, the same method was taken with respect to (1), (5), (6), and (7) of the market-oriented type. The overall points were calculated in the same manner by taking the following into account: (1) economic environment (such as per capita GNP; weight: 10 percent); (2) industrial infrastructure (such as supply of energy; weight: 15 percent); (3) availability of resources (such as iron ore; weight: 25 percent).

As for marks for overall assessments in the case of investments of the market-oriented type, Grade AA was given to those with marks of 76 or more, Grade A to those between 67 and 76, Grade B to those between 62 and 67, Grade C to those between 55 and 62, and Grade D for those less than 55. As for the resources and processing type, Grade AA was given to those with marks of more than 80, Grade A to those between 65 and 80, Grade B to those between 57 and 65, Grade C to those between 50 and 57, and Grade D to those below 50.

26. C. A. Gebelein, C. E. Pearson, and M. Silbergh, "Assessing Political Risk to Foreign Oil Investment Ventures" (Paper presented at the 1977 Society of Petroleum Engineers' Economics and Evaluation Symposium, Dallas, Texas, February 21, 1977).

27. Ibid., p. 1.

28. Ibid., p. 2.

Chapter 5

1. Bayes's rule is a restatement of the rule for conditional probability:

$$P(A \cap B) = P(B/A) \times P(A) = P(A/B) \times P(B).$$

Dividing by $P(A)$ yields:

$$P(B/A) = \frac{P(A/B) \times P(B)}{P(A)},$$

or, if there are numerous *B* events,

$$P(B_i/A) = \frac{P(A/B_i) \times P(B_i)}{\displaystyle\sum_{i=1}^{n} P(A/B_i) \times P(B_i)}$$

where

A is an event

B_i is one of a set of *n* mutually exclusive hypotheses

$P(B_i)$ is the starting, or "prior," probability of a hypothesis

$P(B_i/A)$ is the probability of a hypothesis given *E*, the "revised" probability of a hypothesis, given that a particular event has occured

$P(B/A)$ is the probability of an event given H_i of an event occurring, given a particular underlying cause.

Bayes's rule can be used to reflect experience and calculate the new probability $P(B_i/A)$. Thus,

$$P(B_i/A) = \frac{P(A/B_1) + P(B_1)}{P(A/B_1) \times P(B_1) + P(A/B_2) \times P(B_2)}$$

2. Shiv K. Gupta and John M. Cozzolino, *Fundamentals of Operations Research for Management* (San Francisco: Holden-Day, 1974), pp. 186-187.

3. Nicholas Schweitzer, "Bayesian Analysis for Intelligence: Some Focus on the Middle East" (Paper delivered at the International Studies Association meeting, Toronto, Canada, February 1976).

4. It should be noted that the sum of these probabilities can exceed 100 percent.

5. Alan C. Shapiro, "Capital Budgeting for the Multinational Corporation" (Paper, The Wharton School, University of Pennsylvania, Philadelphia, May 1977).

6. Net present value (NPV) = Inflow – Outflow. The NPV is discounted as follows:

$$NPV = \left[\frac{I_1}{(1+d)^1} + \frac{I_2}{(1+d)^2} + \ldots + \frac{I_n}{(1+d)^n} \right] - \left[O_0 + \frac{O_1}{(1+d)^1} + \ldots + \frac{O_n}{(1+d)^n} \right]$$

7. The number 3.7908 is the appropriate discount factor found in a table for five years at 10 percent discount. We can also calculate as follows:

$$\frac{50}{(1.10)^1} + \frac{50}{(1.10)^2} + \frac{50}{(1.10)^3} + \frac{50}{(1.10)^4} + \frac{50}{(1.10)^5} = \$189.54 \text{ million}$$

8. The figure 2.4356 is the discount factor for 30 percent discount for five years. We can also calculate as follows:

$$\frac{50}{(1.30)^1} + \frac{50}{(1.30)^2} + \frac{50}{(1.30)^3} + \frac{50}{(1.30)^4} + \frac{50}{(1.30)^5} = \$121.78 \text{ million}$$

9. The figure 3.1699 is the appropriate discount factor for four years at 10 percent. We can also calculate as follows:

$$\frac{50}{(1.10)^1} + \frac{50}{(1.10)^2} + \frac{50}{(1.10)^3} + \frac{50}{(1.10)^4} + \frac{0}{(1.10)^5} = \$158.49 \text{ million}$$

The zero amount reflects the expected value in Year 5. Since we are assuming expropriation with no compensation, the expected value for that year is zero.

10. 0.6 x \$50 million = \$30 million.

11. As noted earlier, these conditional probabilities do not have to equal one because the two conditions are not mutually exclusive. For example, the host government may be passing these laws for reasons having nothing to do with a contemplated expropriation.

12. 0.4 x \$50 million = \$20 million.

Chapter 6

1. Jack N. Behrman, *National Interests and the Multinational Enterprise* (Englewood Cliffs, N.J.: Prentice-Hall, 1970).

2. Margaret Kelly, "Evaluating the Risk of Expropriation," *Risk Management*, January 1974, p. 24.

3. Ibid.

4. Stefan H. Robock and Kenneth Simmonds, *International Business and Multinational Enterprises* (Homewood, Ill.: Richard D. Irwin, 1973), pp. 370-375.

5. Bruce Lloyd, "The Identification and Assessment of Political Risk," *Moorgate and Wall Street*, Spring 1975, p. 51. See also Bruce Lloyd, *Political Risk Management* (London: Keith Shipton Developments, Ltd., 1976).

6. Lloyd, "The Identification and Assessment of Political Risk," p. 52.

7. Ibid., p. 53.

8. See also Henry P. de Vries, "Diplomatic Protection of Investments in Foreign Countries," *Columbia Journal of World Business*, September-October 1969.

9. Fred Greene, "The Management of Political Risk," *Bests Review*, July 1974.

10. Seymour J. Rubin, "Transnational Corporations: Supervision, Regulation, or What?" *The International Trade Law Journal*, Spring 1975.

11. We will not deal with exchange risk in this work: much literature is already available on the subject, and there is the question of whether exchange risk should in fact be viewed as political risk.

12. Most of these questions are raised by Lloyd, "The Identification and Assessment of Political Risk," pp. 71-73.

13. Ibid.

14. David G. Bradley, "Managing Against Expropriation," *Harvard Business Review*, July-August 1977, pp. 75-83. For an excellent discussion of the politics of expropriation, see Jessica Pernitz Einhorn, *Expropriation Politics* (Lexington, Mass.: D. C. Heath and Co., 1974).

15. Bradley, "Managing against Expropriation," p. 78.

16. Ibid., p. 79.

17. See Theodore H. Moran, *Multinational Corporations and the Politics of Dependence: Copper in Chile* (Princeton: Princeton University Press, 1974).

18. Bradley, "Managing against Expropriation."

19. For details, see Louis T. Wells, "Social Cost/Benefit Analysis for MNCs," special report, *Harvard Business Review*, March-April 1975.

20. Franklin R. Root, *International Trade and Investment* (Cincinnati: South-Western Publishing Co., 1973).

21. Louis T. Wells, Jr., "Negotiating with Third World Governments," *Harvard Business Review*, January-February 1977.

Chapter 7

1. See Gurney Breckenfeld, "Multinationals at Bay: Coping with the Nation-State," *Saturday Review*, January 24, 1976.

2. See, for example, John Diebold, "Multinational Corporations: Why Be Scared of Them?" *Foreign Policy*, Fall 1973.

3. As quoted in Rawleigh Warner, Jr., "What Doth It Profit a Man," *Saturday Review*, January 24, 1976, p. 20.

4. Joseph LaPalombara and Stephen Blank, *Multinational Corporations and National Elites: A Study in Tensions* (New York: The Conference Board, 1976). See also idem, *Multinational Corporations in Comparative Perspective* (New York: The Conference Board, 1977).

5. *Terrorism* (1977) is highly recommended as an excellent international journal on the subject. The Center for Strategic and International Studies, Washington, D.C., hosted a conference on "Terrorism and U.S. Business" on December 14, 1977.

6. Jacqueline Grapin, "French Hostility toward Business," *Washington Post*, April 15, 1978, p. A-11.

7. Julian Radcliffe, "Political Risk Insurance Market Expands," *Risk Management*, April 1974.

8. Ted Gurr, *Politimetrics: An Introduction to Quantitative Macropolitics* (Englewood Cliffs, N.J.: Prentice-Hall, 1972), has defined politimetrics as "the quantitative study of political groups, institutions, nations and international systems. It is a way of doing research whose common object is to identify, measure and explain regularities in the properties and dynamics of political entities."

Appendix A

1. See, for example, Talcott Parsons, *The Social System* (New York: Free Press, 1953); David Easton, *A Framework for Political Analysis* (Englewood Cliffs, N.J.: Prentice-Hall, 1965); idem, *A Systems Analysis of Political Life* (New York: John Wiley and Sons, 1965); and James Coleman and Gabriel Almond, *The Politics of the Developing Areas* (Princeton: Princeton University Press, 1960).

2. The countries were Antigua, Barbados, Belize, Botswana, the Republic of China, Dominica, Gambia, Lesotho, Mauritius, St. Catherine-Nevis-Anguilla, St. Lucia, St. Vincent, Singapore, and Western Samoa.

3. The authors of *Overseas Investment and Political Risk* worked on several large projects that involved the use of quantitative data on the nation-state level. These included studies on twenty Latin American countries, eighty-five LDCs, twenty-five LDCs that have experienced guerrilla insurgencies, and fifteen Caribbean countries. We also conducted qualitative analyses of political and economic developments in Latin America, the Arab world, South Asia, and sub-Saharan Africa. For countries on which we did not have direct knowledge, the expertise of other staff members of the Foreign Policy Research Institute was tapped. The material contained in this appendix is from the monograph.

4. This *Atlas Narodov Mira* Index is contained in Charles Taylor and Michael Hudson, *World Handbook of Political and Social Indicators*, 2d ed. (New Haven: Yale University Press, 1972).

5. Data on percentage growth in GNP for the years 1960-1965 were taken from ibid. Data on energy consumption were taken from Arthur Banks, *Cross-Polity Times-Series Data* (Cambridge, Mass.: MIT Press, 1971).

6. Ted Gurr, "Psychological Factors in Civil Violence," *World Politics*, January 1968, pp. 245-278.

7. Raymond Tanter and Manus Midlarsky, "A Theory of Revolution," *Journal of Conflict Resolution* 2 (1967).

8. See, for example, Rudy Rummel, "Dimensions of Conflict Behavior Within and Between Nations," in *General Systems Yearbook* 8 (1963); Raymond Tanter, "Dimensions of Conflict Behavior Within Nations, 1955-1960; Turmoil and Internal War," *Peace Research Society Papers* 3 (1965); Gerald T. West, "The Dimensions of Political Violence in Latin America, 1949-1964: An Empirical Study" (Ph.D. diss., University of Pennsylvania, 1973); U.S., Central Intelligence Agency, *Profile of Violence: An Analytical Model* (Washington, D.C.: Central Intelligence Agency, June 1976).

9. The data on demonstrations and government crises were from Banks, *Cross-Polity Time Series Data*. The data on riots were from Taylor and Hudson, *World Handbook*. See both sources for complete definitions and data collection procedures.

10. The data on guerrilla warfare, coups, and assassinations were taken from Banks, *Cross-Polity Times Series Data*. The data on armed attacks were taken from Taylor and Hudson, *World Handbook*. See both sources for complete definitions and data collection procedures.

11. Although it was not empirically tested, it is likely that a correlation exists between the number of men in the armed forces per capita and the number of men in the internal security forces per capita. It would have been redundant, therefore, to use both indicators.

12. The data on the first three variables were from Banks, *Cross-Polity Time Series Data*. The data on irregular executive changes were taken from Taylor and Hudson, *World Handbook*.

13. The scoring of each of these variables is fully described in Banks, *Cross-Polity Time Series Data*, p. xxii.

14. It should be noted that the overlap between this variable and the coup d'etat indicator, which is a component of the Internal Violence Index, is less than it appears. The coup indicator includes both successful and unsuccessful attempts, but the irregular executive change variable includes only successful attempts. In view of the significance of

a coup or an irregular executive change for the stability of a political system, a dual counting of such events was deemed appropriate.

Appendix B

1. U.S., Department of State, Bureau of Intelligence and Research, report no. 799, May 18, 1977, prepared by Dianne Markowitz.

2. Combined total for war, expropriation, and inconvertibility coverages.

3. OPIC has been directed to turn its insurance programs over to the private sector by 1981 and to act solely as a reinsurer after that time.

4. Investment data obtained from the Development Assistance Committee of the Organization for Economic Cooperation and Development.

5. Until January 1977, OPIC issued only very narrow coverage in the petroleum sector (tangible and removable assets). If the petroleum sector, which accounts for some 20 percent of U.S. investment in LDCs, were excluded from U.S. investment statistics, OPIC's percentage would rise to about 14 percent. OPIC's new program for coverage in this sector is still in the formative stage, and applications are being considered on a case-by-case basis.

Index

Moran, Theodore, 16, 18
Müller, Ronald, 27

New International Economic Order,
   19, 22
Nikkei Business Ranking, 114, 116-
   119

Organization for Economic Cooper-
   ation and Development, 20-22
Overseas Investment Insurance
   Group, 60-62, 67
Overseas Private Investment Corpo-
   ration, 3-12, 28, 30, 33-69, 154-155

Peru, 8, 28, 66
Political Risk, definition, 5, 80-82
Political System Stability Index, 106,
   107, 109, 154

Raw Materials, 1, 5, 7, 31, 50, 69
Restrictive Business Practices, 23
Revere Copper and Brass, 28

Robock, Stefan, 73, 76-79, 80
Root, Franklin, 16, 73-75, 80, 136

Senate Committee on Foreign Rela-
   tions, 63-67
Senate Subcommittee on Multina-
   tional Corporations, 44-50, 54
Shell Oil model, 114, 120-124
South Africa, 1
Stobaugh, Robert, 93, 96

Truitt, Frederick, 15, 16

United Nations Commission on
   Transnational Corporations, 22
United States Congress, 3, 9, 17, 20,
   59, 69
United States government, 2, 4, 8, 20,
   21, 24, 26, 33-69, 94
Uruguay, 8

Wheelock, Keith, 44
Willett, Alan, 83